The Western Guide to Feng Shui for Romance

HAY HOUSE TITLES
OF RELATED INTEREST

Books

FENG SHUI FOR THE SOUL, by Denise Linn
SPACE CLEARING A–Z, by Denise Linn

The above are available at your local bookstore, or may be
ordered by visiting: Hay House USA: **www.hayhouse.com**
Hay House Australia: **www.hayhouse.com.au**
Hay House UK: **www.hayhouse.co.uk**
Hay House South Africa: **orders@psdprom.co.za**

THE WESTERN GUIDE TO

Feng Shui

for

Romance

THE DANCE

OF HEART

& HOME

Terah Kathryn Collins

HAY HOUSE, INC.
Carlsbad, California
London • Sydney • Johannesburg
Vancouver • Hong Kong

Published and distributed in the United States by: Hay House, Inc., P.O. Box 5100, Carlsbad, CA 92018-5100 • *Phone:* (760) 431-7695 or (800) 654-5126 • *Fax:* (760) 431-6948 or (800) 650-5115 • www.hayhouse.com • **Published and distributed in Australia by:** Hay House Australia Ltd., 18/36 Ralph St., Alexandria NSW 2015 • *Phone:* 612-9669-4299 • *Fax:* 612-9669-4144 • www.hayhouse.com.au • **Published and distributed in the United Kingdom by:** Hay House UK, Ltd. • Unit 202, Canalot Studios • 222 Kensal Rd., London W10 5BN • *Phone:* 44-20-8962-1230 • *Fax:* 44-20-8962-1239 • www.hayhouse.co.uk • **Published and distributed in the Republic of South Africa by:** Hay House SA (Pty), Ltd., P.O. Box 990, Witkoppen 2068 • *Phone/Fax:* 2711-7012233 • orders@psdprom.co.za • **Distributed in Canada by:** Raincoast • 9050 Shaughnessy St., Vancouver, B.C. V6P 6E5 • *Phone:* (604) 323-7100 • *Fax:* (604) 323-2600

Editorial supervision: Jill Kramer   *Design:* Jenny Richards
Cover and Interior illustrations: Eris Klein

Library of Congress Cataloging-in-Publication Data

Collins, Terah Kathryn.
  The western guide to feng shui for romance : the dance of heart and home / Terah Kathryn Collins.
     p. cm.
  ISBN 1-56170-814-3 (Hardcover)
  1. Man-woman relationships. 2. Feng shui. I. Title.
  HQ801.C693 2004
  306.7—dc21

                                                          2003012572

                              ISBN 1-56170-814-3

                        07 06 05 04   4 3 2 1
                        1st printing, January 2004

                  Printed in the United States of America

To Alice Marie and
Whitwell Torre.

With love
and gratitude.

CONTENTS

Foreword

HOME IMPROVEMENT MEETS THE TWILIGHT ZONE

WHEN MY WIFE, Terah, asked me to write the Foreword for this, her fifth book, one question came immediately to mind: Why me? What could I possibly explain, that she or one of her Feng Shui buddies couldn't explain better?

"A guy's point of view on romance and Feng Shui," Terah explained. "Particularly an engineer-type guy like you."

I got it. My background includes nuclear physics, engineering, the Naval Academy, and 13 years in the military. She figured that my perspective would be helpful to all of the guys out there who wonder, *What is this Feng Shui stuff, anyway?*

Let me say that I received my "Foundational Feng Shui Training" in the Navy's

Submarine Service. The saying "A place for everything and everything in its place" wasn't just a suggestion, it was an order! As tight as submarine space was, we couldn't have functioned in any other way. There was no time to look for things—we had to know immediately where everything was. Clearing clutter was supercritical in my military experience. And, from a Feng Shui perspective, it's also crucial in our everyday lives as well.

With this training under my belt, I had the neatness thing down pat, but I was lacking in the romance department. When Terah and I first got together, my bedroom was really my home office, with a single bed against the far wall. There were no decorations except over the bed, where I'd hung an ornate crucifix left over from my Catholic upbringing. Now a crucifix is a meaningful religious symbol to some, but it really didn't bring a lot of warmth and romance into my bedroom. When Terah said, "Tell me about this . . . why did you choose this particular location for a crucifix?" I was forced to admit that when I moved in, that's where the nail was. (It's a guy thing.) She suggested that I move the nail and the crucifix, make my guest room into the office, and get a bigger bed. She also explained that my bedroom was in the area of my apartment that related to Love and Marriage. I can look back now and see that when I spruced it up with some art and flowers (and a larger bed), my romance with Terah—and a whole new lifestyle—began.

At first, our courtship was like *Home Improvement* (me) meeting *The Twilight Zone* (her). And Feng Shui . . . come on! If I couldn't see it, put it to a double-blind test, and treat it like a science experiment, I wasn't going to swallow it.

Then an interesting thing happened. Terah's first book came out, with our home phone as a contact point. And boy, did we get calls! Tearful, joyful, relieved calls, "Your book changed my life" calls and "Where can I learn more about this?" calls. This was empirical proof—in the field, statistical proof. People who'd lost all hope, people who didn't even really believe in Feng Shui, people with no vested interest in this "experiment" working—they were all getting results.

We also received letters. This is a direct quote from the first one: "You saved my life." And there were dozens just like it. My proof was arriving, and I was becoming a believer.

So for the disbelievers reading this, just know that you're in for some changes . . . good ones. And if I might "bottom-line" it for you, here's my guy's version of Feng Shui. If you just do these three things, you're 90 percent there:

1. Pick up after yourself; organize your stuff in the garage, basement, closet, or wherever you've stashed it; and get rid of all the old crap you'll never use or need again.

2. Follow instructions in the "Lifestyle and Home Balance Analyses" chapter in this book.

3. Close the lid on the damn toilet!

These tips will do wonders for your love life . . . and your happiness quotient.

And for those of you trying to get these points across to your mate, don't give up. I've found that Feng Shui makes for smooth relationships, which makes for happy people and a happy home. It's worked that way for me, and it can work that way for you, too.

— Brian Collins

Terah and Brian

Preface

GARDEN
OF
EARTHLY
DELIGHTS

LOOKING BACK, IT all makes perfect sense. In early 1990, I left the house that my second husband and I shared in San Diego and moved into a studio cottage with a private garden. Located a block from the ocean, the garden and cottage were the same size— 450 square feet each—creating a perfectly balanced indoor-outdoor space. It was my Garden of Earthly Delights, so named by Brian Collins, the man I'd eventually leave it for. But first, I'd launch my Feng Shui practice, discover the connection between my unfortunate love life and my choices in housing, and learn to swim in the warm waters of self-love.

Just about everyone who experiences a disruption of the heart and home asks, "What happened?"

and "Where did I go wrong?" It's in our nature to do some soul searching when love, the guiding light that once filled our hearts and deliv-
ered us to the altar of loving commitment, blinks out. Soul searching
also occurs in the minds of people who wish they had a lover, or who
have a lover they're unhappy with. Search as we might, our self-inquiry
can still leave many questions unanswered. Feng Shui observes that
answers—revelations—can be found when we widen our search to
include an "environmental inquiry" of our surroundings. Here, a whole
new world is revealed that can identify imbalances that were always
present if we'd had the eyes to see them. When we can see clearly
how the environment is holding what we *don't* want in place and take
the initiative to correct it, we take a powerful step into the heart and
home of happiness.

From a Feng Shui perspective, it's fascinating to mentally revisit the
houses I've inhabited. My Feng Shui eyes can clearly see the homes'
"splinters," or imbalances that helped hold a mediocre or negative situation in place. I remember that my first husband and I lived in an
L-shaped house that was missing the area related to love and marriage
(described in detail in Appendix A). Unknowingly, we exacerbated the
house's imbalance by accentuating the white walls and cobalt-blue carpeting with furnishings and decor in the same colors. The house felt as

cold as a walk-in freezer, but at the time we thought it was "cool" to make everything match. Looking back, I can see that the house's shape and the unrelenting blue-and-white palette discouraged romance and intimacy. With no "home fires burning," we soon became irrevocably estranged, and parted ways.

Just as we know that certain conditions and challenges can compromise our bodies, Feng Shui observes that the same holds true in our homes. I recall the environmental conditions present in the house I shared with my second husband. Our master bedroom was "stylishly" designed to give a commanding view of the bathroom from the bed. His side of the bed was graced with the *primary* view of the toilet (which was left open all the time), while I looked directly into the gaping shower stall and a large planter box full of waterlogged plants. If I could have read the Feng Shui interpretation of this unfavorable location, it would have said:

> *The open toilet, seen first thing in the morning and last thing at night, symbolizes a drain upon your husband's life force. Here, he'll experience depression and feel as if his resources are being flushed away before he can enjoy them. Your view of the shower stall also connotes a drain upon <u>your</u> life force, while the*

WESTERN GUIDE TO FENG SHUI FOR ROMANCE

drowning plants symbolize a steady loss of vitality. These disparate, uninspiring views represent a dissension of vital energy. Here, stress and marital challenges can multiply, as you'll differ more and more in your "points of view" in life.

This interpretation would have been uncannily accurate. However, since I was still illiterate in the language of Feng Shui, I only knew that we were becoming unhappier with every passing day.

My first Feng Shui class with Dr. Richard Tan, an acupuncturist and Feng Shui expert in San Diego, was an epiphany. One of his primary guidelines was to create an inspiring, unified view from the bed that *isn't* of the bathroom. Clearly, our view was "bad Feng Shui," and that wasn't all. The bathroom was in the area of the house related to Love and Marriage, while the Wealth area was located in our dirty, cluttered garage. I felt like I'd just discovered the answer to everything. Our differing points of view were centered on money, and now I knew how to fix it! And fix it I did. Within 24 hours of emptying the planter of unhealthy plants, screening the bathroom from the bed, and cleaning out the garage, we had the "truth talk" we'd been avoiding for more than a year.

The Feng Shui improvements in the house seemed to open us up and give us the strength to face reality. Previously stuck, we were suddenly free to move forward; our words poured out, and everything became crystal clear. He was going in one direction, and I in another, and neither of us wished to compromise. We didn't have children to consider, and we both felt that it was time to let go. That night, we decided that our marriage was over. Thirty days later, I was living in my little Garden of Earthly Delights.

Why didn't my Feng Shui enhancements cause my ex-husband and me to live happily ever after? We *are* living happily ever after, just not with each other! When my Feng Shui handiwork aligned our home to hold happiness in place, we realized that we wished to pursue our happiness separately. For most couples, Feng Shui marks the sweet return of intimate happiness *together,* as romantic conditions are enhanced and splinters are removed or transformed. Such an environmental inquiry also opens the door to a deeper understanding of life. We see that our happiness is anchored by two primary influences: heart—our capacity to love self and others; and home—the environment that surrounds us.

I knew that I had some work to do. I'd moved from a mediocre, disjointed existence into a tiny jewel box that sparkled with possibility. My first conscious step in learning the dance of heart and home was to bring only the possessions containing good memories and feelings into my new house. It wasn't much. Out of a large household of things, I brought a futon, a small desk and two chairs, a few dishes, and my favorite books. Each item glowed with positive associations and anchored my optimistic new beginning in place.

My solitary life gave me the time and space to explore my own rhythms and preferences. I had always depended on a man—father, boyfriend, or husband—to love me, a condition that lacked self-respect and created a mediocre existence that was ruled by others. Here, I was going to open my heart, practice unconditional self-love, and create a romantic life without relying on a man to do it for me or with me!

My cottage became my Feng Shui instrument. I fine-tuned every area, paying special attention to two spots. To symbolize self-love, I made a collage of inspirational images that touched my heart—angels and beautiful natural places—and hung it in my "Love and Marriage" bathroom, which, fortunately, was quite private and beautiful. I also displayed my Feng Shui books near the cottage's front entrance in the area related to Career. Soon, I noticed a remarkable change in myself.

The abject terror of public speaking that had paralyzed me in the past was dissipating, and I began to give talks on Feng Shui at local venues. It was at one of these lectures that I met best-selling author Louise Hay, the founder and publisher of Hay House, who would soon say to me, "You'd better be writing this stuff down, honey. We want to publish a book on Feng Shui, and you have first crack at it. What do you say: yes or no?"

I said yes.

That was one of the two life-changing blessings I said yes to during that time. The second blessing was born out of a quiet moment and a box of collected treasures. I was sifting through my small collection and enjoying all the memories that these bits of jewelry, photos, and keepsakes brought to mind. I threaded my hand through the top of a wind chime made of iridescent glass bells and gently raised them to the window. The breeze sent them singing, a delicate sweet sound—so like wedding bells, I mused. Wedding bells. Was I ready to even consider the possibility? I answered the question by hanging the bells in the bathroom window with a promise and a knowing that only the love of my life would be able to hear such a sweet sound.

Within two weeks of hanging those bells, Brian Collins galloped up to my door, all sunshine and gentlemanly grace. My biggest challenge was to accept the gift. *Wasn't he just a little too sunny, and a bit too nice,* asked a voice I recognized as my own from the past? No! He was different from any man I'd ever met. He was the love of my life come calling. He was the one who named my garden cottage the Garden of Earthly Delights, and who romanced me out of it a year later.

We're now married and live in a house that came with its own set of Feng Shui challenges and that we've had great fun transforming to hold our happiness in place. There's a delicious feeling that comes from making a house into a "personal paradise," where the dance of heart and home can elegantly unfold, and where intimacy and happiness can thrive.

That's what this book is all about. It will help you stage a life that's a magnet for happiness, a place where your dreams can come true. Enjoy your Feng Shui discoveries and the romantic adventures that are sure to follow. Fall in love with yourself, and embrace what makes your heart—and your home—sing.

— Terah Kathryn Collins

ACKNOWLEDGMENTS

Special thanks to:

Laurel and Matthew Aarsvold
Marilyn Adams
Carol and Klint Beatson
Diane and Juan Carrillo
Karen Carrasco
Rita Cofrancesco
Jennie and David Cornsweet
Barbra Dillenger and Michael Makay
Jackee and Richard Earnest
Gabriella and Juan Flores
Gita Gendloff and Sand Miller
Louise Hay
Rhonda Karp and Dan Cool
Liv Kellgren
Shivam Kohls and Steve Tomae
Marylou LoPreste and Craig Perkins
Becky Lott and Raymond Egan
Barbara Masters and Alan Richards
Mary McNolte and Gary Walker
Marti and Ron Montbleau

Christiane Northrup
Jane and Bill Ozuna
Karen and Gary Pooler
Francina and Neil Prince
Cheryl Rice
Ellen and Eric Schneider
Dale and Blanca Schusterman
Terri Stark
Barbara Takashima and Dan McFarland
Ron Tillinghast
Reid Tracy
Greg Verhey

. . . for your invaluable feedback and loving support.

PART I

THE DANCE OF HEART & HOME

FENG SHUI, the study of arranging your environment to enhance your life, is all about happiness. And ultimately, what is happiness without romance? Here, romance is viewed not as a fleeting fancy, but an ongoing and deeply satisfying lifestyle that's self-generated. It's born out of the elegant dance between your inner and outer worlds, a dance that unites your heart and home in an intimate partnership that causes all heaven to break loose in your life. To master this dance, you learn to honor your own rhythms, pursue the interests that fuel your passions, and make lifestyle choices that deeply anchor your happiness in place. You treat yourself with the same tender, loving kindness that you would a lover. Such an internal love affair, partnered with your loving attention to your environment, is the foundation upon which real happiness is built, and the magnet that attracts all good things, including romance, to your door.

1.

Chapter 1

THE ETERNAL ROMANCE OF MADAM YIN AND MASTER YANG

IN FENG SHUI, balance—the harmonious interplay between opposite forces—is the key to creating happiness. These opposite forces are called Yin and Yang, and they define the dual nature of our entire universe. The happiness you strive for—or currently enjoy—is inherent in the delightful "just right" balance between Yin and Yang extremes. You're continually defining your preferences and making adjustments to strike such a balance in your everyday life. Think of the difference between taking a nice warm shower versus a scalding or freezing one, sitting in a beautifully lit room versus one that's blindingly bright or pitch black, or participating in a friendly conversation versus stony silence or a loud argument.

Happiness thrives in the human-friendly conditions of harmony, comfort, pleasure, and beauty—conditions we enjoy when we know how to balance the Yin and Yang qualities of our lives.

Whether you're a woman or a man, you'll find that *both* Yin and Yang qualities abound within and around you. They're *not* gender specific. The strongest, most masculine man in the world has qualities associated with the classically feminine Yin. When he's a dad who likes to spend quality time with his kids, a lover who's sensitive and considerate, or a craftsman who keeps his tools clean and organized, he's revealing his Yin side.

Likewise, the most delicate, feminine woman expresses her masculine Yang side in her fast-paced career, her ability to run ten errands at a time, and her industrious participation in a multitude of activities. So, the female and male, the beloved and lover, the goddess and god, are forever intertwined within each of us, no matter what our sex or sexual persuasion may be. With this in mind, let's breathe life into the world of Yin and Yang and explore how they manifest within and around us.

Meet Madam Yin, the Queen of Serenity. She's the keeper of your tranquility, the guardian of your daily rest, the mother of your intuition. Stillness in all its forms—meditation, daydreaming, lounging, and sleep—are all in her domain. Her leisurely pace invites you *in and down*, where you can fully receive all the subtle, sweet nuances that life has to offer. She's the diva of the orderly care of things, knowing that order maintains peace of mind. Her magnetic presence resides in all that is calm and comfortable—the overstuffed reading chair, the bed laden with downy linens, the soft window seat overlooking a shady garden, a sanctuary glowing in the candlelight, a leisurely bath. Her sensual nature is found in all the lovely touches that make a house a home: the bowl of juicy, ripe fruit, the voluptuous bouquet of flowers, the simmering soup, the plate of cookies, and the many other earthly pleasures that cause you to breathe in deeply and say, "Ahh, yes . . ."

Now Master Yang . . . he's the King of Action. His nonstop pace moves you *up and out,* igniting your excitement and enthusiasm to go, go, go! He's the wild initiator of speed and adventure, surging through life at a fast, often chaotic pace. His dynamic movement forward animates all that is "on the wing"—the weekday morning rush in the kitchen, a rowdy celebration with friends, the quick-witted repartee with colleagues, the music that whirls you out of your seat, and the many activities that can keep you up half the night. He is expressed in all that's bright and dramatic in a home—the huge, dazzling mirror; an oversized crimson couch; a long slab of brightly polished stone across the mantel; and all the flashy, bigger-than-life things that make you exclaim, "Oh wow!"

Madam Yin, goddess of comfort, leisure, and sensuality, is quintessentially receptive to the sweet pleasures of life, charming you into savoring the moment. Master Yang, god of every kind of passion, is pure, potent vitality—awakening your lust for life with heat and intensity. You experience their romantic union when you're happily engaged in life, with just the right mix of delightful stimulation and deeply restorative leisure.

Oh, but how quickly they can lose their balance! All you need is to really be in a hurry, and Master Yang exerts his force and takes over, pushing the calm and orderly Madam Yin aside. The more you make haste and crowd activities together, the faster he goes. Eventually, overexertion causes utter depletion and collapse. In the end, Master Yang is always forced to return to Madam Yin, but his frantically paced jaunt without her is never a very pleasant one. Happiness comes when they share the daily journey of life together as intimate partners.

Coming Back to Our Senses

The primary imbalance found in our Western world today has to do with the glorification of Master Yang. By and large, he rules our lifestyle and lords over Madam Yin, impatiently dismissing her common-sense cues to relax and slow down. Evidence of this can be seen in the huge popularity of coffee, colas, and other "speedy" caffeine drinks; long, demanding school and work weeks; short vacations packed with activities; the predominance of fast-food restaurants; and the passion for action movies, electronics, sports, and fast cars. In the extreme, Yang conditions are evident in communities of people who are too busy to know their neighbors, feel entitled to instant gratification, are aggressive, and who disregard others in their perpetual haste.

The domination of Master Yang is understandable. Any historical account includes the lament of how long it took to travel, distribute goods, and send and receive communications. Centuries have been ruled by the slow earthiness of Madam Yin. But those times are past. Our Western culture is now the benefactor of speed. After an eternity of slow going, we've leaped into a pace that quickens with every passing day. The pendulum has swung from one extreme to the other, and whenever one side is left behind, unhappiness results, and the quest for balance begins. We pine for the missing qualities the other partner brings to life, and look for ways to regain equilibrium.

This is evident in the current popularity of "altars to Madam Yin." She's being reinstated in the sumptuous spa bathrooms, sanctuaries, lounging areas, reading nooks, and other private "rooms of your own" that are so in vogue now. The burgeoning interest in earth-friendly building and natural-health practices, as well as in organizing and creating sacred space in our homes and workplaces, carries our wish to soothe the manic Master Yang. We experience their reconciliation when we bask in the sights, sounds, tastes, smells, and feelings we love; fully appreciate our connection with heaven *and* Earth; cherish our relationships with others; and take delight in practicing "random kindness and senseless acts of beauty."

To create a pleasurable, passionate lifestyle, establishing equality between Yin and Yang is key. Master Yang is always happiest when he embraces the many sensual pleasures Madam Yin has to offer. Conversely, she's refreshed and uplifted by his passionate enthusiasm. Together, they elegantly sweep, bend, and flex to life's ever-changing music. Wooed by each other's charms, they inevitably fall in love, and as the fantasy comes true, they live happily ever after within you. And, inevitably, such an internal love affair attracts others of like heart into your life.

Chapter 2

LIFESTYLE AND HOME BALANCE ANALYSES

FENG SHUI PAYS close attention to your lifestyle choices as well as to your home environment, as they show where adjustments can be made to achieve the Yin/Yang balance that anchors your happiness in place.

Lifestyle Balance Analysis

Take a few moments to score yourself 1 to 5 on both sides of the following list to determine the Yin and Yang influences in your current lifestyle. If your weekdays are very different from your weekends, score your lifestyle from a weekday perspective, and then score it again from a weekend perspective to see how they compare.

1 - Rarely or never • 2 - Sometimes • 3 - About half the time
4 - Often • 5 - Very often or always

The predominant way I live my life is to:

Yin	Yang
___Spend a lot of time at home	___Spend a lot of time away from home
___Rest/sleep/nap	___Work/be active
___Give time to myself	___Give time to others
___Work alone	___Work with other people
___Hang out alone	___Socialize and entertain
___Have quiet, intimate conversations	___Have loud, animated conversations
___Meditate, write in a journal, reflect	___Move, dance, exercise
___Read silently	___Read aloud
___Lounge around	___Do chores
___Speak softly	___Speak loudly
___Listen more than talk	___Talk more than listen
___Feel grounded	___Feel spacey
___Feel relaxed	___Feel stressed
___Feel calm	___Feel excited
___Drink decaffeinated beverages	___Drink caffeinated beverages
___Prepare home-cooked meals	___Eat prepared foods
___Dine leisurely	___Eat on the run
___Take a relaxing bath	___Take a quick shower
___Leave in plenty of time	___Rush to be on time
___Be organized	___Be disorganized
___Do one thing at a time	___Do many things at a time
___Drive at the speed limit	___Drive faster than the speed limit
___Engage in quiet pastimes	___Engage in lively activities
___Listen to relaxing music	___Listen to loud music
___Relax in the garden	___Work in the garden
___Get a full night's sleep	___Go to bed late and get up early

12   TOTAL: ____ **Yin**   ____ **Yang**

A balanced lifestyle will show up in scores that are approximately the same on each side of the list. If you find that your score is currently very high on one side and low on the other, choose pastimes or activities suggested on the low side of the list to strike a new balance. When doing so, be sure to choose the things that you really enjoy. For instance, if you need more Yin pastimes to balance your Yang lifestyle, you may decide to dine more leisurely in the evenings, while someone else would much rather set time aside in the mornings for quiet introspection.

Some people find that their combined weekday and weekend scores create an overall balance in their lifestyle. These are men and women who've discovered how to be "King or Queen for a day" (or two) each week. They completely relax, recoup, and immerse themselves in a Yin atmosphere to balance a very Yang-oriented workweek. They know how to reverse their gears and dive down into the pure sensual pleasures of leisure—with no errands, no frenetic activities, no hurrying along. This rhythm can work well to balance one extreme with the other.

Being too long in the Yang mode, however, can still produce an imbalance, even when there's a vacation to look forward to. If every single day requires a lot of activity, include an hour or more of restorative time daily, knowing that your health and happiness depend on it.

On the other hand, there are people who've been shut in with Madam Yin too long. Many senior citizens feel they've been "left behind" as the lives of younger friends and family members go whirring quickly past them. Pulled in and down by too much stillness, they wish for some excitement to whisk them up, up, and away.

Even when there are physical or other limitations, it's vital to get out into the world for a little stimulation. If you find that your life has become stagnant and uneventful, invite Master Yang to gallop in for the rescue. Consider taking classes at a local community center, reading to children at the library, or volunteering at a hospital or animal shelter. Start a club that focuses on a special interest such as reading, cooking, or traveling. Plan a trip by ship, train, bus, or plane and go somewhere you've always wanted to go. In almost every case, there

are many enjoyable ways in which you can attain the healthy balance you're looking for.

It's interesting to notice how you can blend Yin and Yang influences to reset your balance. This is where you can show off your fancier steps in the dance of balancing your lifestyle. For instance, a race-walk with a friend is quite different from a meandering stroll alone. Both involve walking, but the first example includes the Yang qualities of speedy, directed movement and conversation, while the second allows for a slower Yin pace and quiet solitude.

If your day has involved a hundred conversations and a lot of activity, your balance would most likely be found in the slower, quieter walk. On the other hand, if you'd been sitting alone all day, the faster, chattier walk would be the perfect choice. Become a keen observer of the Yin-Yang portions of your life, and enjoy the endless ways in which you can elegantly step right back into balance.

Home Balance Analysis

As an "environmental body," your home supports and encourages your current lifestyle. If you're living in the lap of happiness now, your home is doing a good job of holding your happiness in place. If you're not happy, there are probably some imbalances in your home that are anchoring your unhappiness in place.

A home is balanced when it has the just-right combination of Yin Quiet Zones and Yang Active Zones that support a happy lifestyle:

YIN QUIET ZONES	YANG ACTIVE ZONES
Bedroom	Living room
Bathroom	Kitchen
Dining room	Family or great room
Sanctuary	Home office
Storage areas	Laundry room

Use the following list to assess your home (or workplace) room by room to determine the current balance of each space. If you have equal amounts of a given feature in a room, such as both small and large art, circle both. If there's a category that doesn't exist in a room, simply move to the next one.

Name of the room _____

	Yin ♥ Yang
Room size	Small ♥ Large
Location in house	Quiet, private ♥ Noisy, busy
Room's view	Intimate-private ♥ Grand
Room's view	Natural ♥ Houses, buildings, street
Ceiling	Low ♥ High
Natural light	Low ♥ Bright
Electrical light	Dim ♥ Bright
Open floor space	Small amounts ♥ Large expanses
Floors	Dark or ornate ♥ Light or plain
Wall colors	Medium, dark, or muted ♥ Light or bright

cont'd. on next page

	Yin ♥ Yang
Furniture	Many pieces ♥ Few pieces
Furniture colors	Medium, dark, or muted ♥ Light or bright
Furniture and decor	Small ♥ Large
Furniture and decor	Low ♥ High
Seating	Soft, padded ♥ Hard, unpadded
Furniture shapes	Curved, rounded lines ♥ Straight, angular lines
Patterns	Floral ♥ Geometric
Fabrics	Textured ♥ Smooth, shiny
Design	Elaborate, layered, ornate ♥ Plain, uncomplicated
Displayed collections	Many ♥ Few or none
Art	Many pieces ♥ Few or no pieces
Art	Small ♥ Large
Pillows	Many ♥ Few or none
Books	Many ♥ Few or none
Mirrors	Small ♥ Large
Plants	Many ♥ Few or none
Storage areas/closets	Organized ♥ Chaotic, disorganized

TOTAL   _____**Yin**   _____**Yang**

In general, when your home has a predominance of Yang features and your lifestyle is unrelentingly active, introduce Yin elements to achieve balance, particularly in the quiet-zone rooms. For instance, accentuate the Yin nature of a bathroom by adorning it with sensual accoutrements that trigger a relaxation response, such as dark, muted colors; plush bath linens; low lighting; scented candles and soaps; and soothing music. Conversely, if you find that your all-too-quiet lifestyle is being held in place by a predominantly Yin house, add Yang features, especially in the active zone rooms of the house. Turn the lights up, remove some of the knickknacks, add bright or light colors, and clear floor space so that you can really move around.

Smooth Moves

Interestingly, many people who live together find that their answers differ according to their tastes and individual sense of size, shape, color, and light. In our case, for example, my husband, Brian, sees three pretty things on the coffee table in our living room as "many," while I see them as "few." Compare notes with the people you live with to better understand how they experience the home you share, and find ways to strike a balance that honors everyone. In our case, we've adorned the coffee table with one orchid plant, and I make more ornate arrangements of my favorite things in my home office.

Variations abound! Adapt the Lifestyle and Home Balance Analyses to fit your own needs and circumstances. For instance, in our household, Brian's home office is a classically Yang powerhouse of activity. It's located at the front of the house where he can easily greet clients. His huge desk wraps around two bright periwinkle walls, and a large mirror gives him a commanding view of the door. A sunny yellow ceiling, large windows, a skylight, and a central spotlight fill the room with light. Filing cabinets and reference materials are stored in the closet, giving the room a clean, minimalist look.

My office is quite the opposite, reflecting my writer's need for

Yin space. It's in the quietest part of the house, with thick area rugs laid over carpeting; a comfortable love seat; shelves full of books and plants; deep earthen-colored walls; eight pretty lamps; and ever-changing arrangements of flowers, photos, and art. It's as much a sanctuary as it is a home office, and it serves me well as both.

With an artful eye and some creative handiwork, you can give every room in your home the kiss of your own personality. And because the dance of heart and home is always in motion, your rooms are at their best when you've arranged them to flex into the needs of the moment. Brian can dim the lights in his office and it becomes a twilight-colored nook for a quiet conversation during a party. Or, I can turn on every lamp in my office, pile my reference materials in chaotic heaps everywhere, and power through a deadline. In the best of all worlds, you become the dancer who elegantly choreographs the balance of Yin and Yang to bring out the best of every moment in every room in your house.

Have fun with this, and enjoy the dance!

Chapter 3

HOLDING
HAPPINESS
IN
PLACE

AS YOUR ENVIRON-
mental body, your home quite literally holds your lifestyle in place. Happiness thrives in a well-balanced home, where Yin and Yang influences each find an inviting place to live.

My client Lori strikes such a balance. She is single, works as a hotel concierge, and lives in a two-bedroom condominium. After a busy day at work, she dives deep into the soothing Yin rituals of journaling and soaking in a candlelit bath. Once a week, she enjoys a deep muscle massage. Her busy work schedule, along with exercising twice a week and socializing with a close circle of friends, satisfies the Yang side of life. Several times a month, she has a "date night" with herself, which includes a glass of wine, an array of favorite snacks, and a good movie. She bathes, puts on something comfy, lights candles, pops in the video, and enjoys a complete time-out.

Her lifestyle is beautifully held in place by the bright comfort of her living room and kitchen; the nurturing atmosphere of her dining area; the sensual appeal of her bathroom, bedroom, and meditation alcove; and the organized elements that comprise the home office in the second bedroom. When asked if she'd like to be in romantically involved, she replied, "I am! I'm taking this time to romance myself, explore my own rhythms, and do the things I love to do. A lover would be wonderful, but I'm having a great time right now."

Because Lori lives alone, it's relatively easy for her to hand-hone a happily balanced lifestyle. But what about people who have a few more variables in their lives? The same rules of balance apply. They just need to be creatively tailored to fit the circumstances.

Clients Anne and Henry come to mind. When I first met them, their lifestyle was ruled by Yang conditions. They had demanding careers that kept them busy all week. Their two children added many activities to their evenings and weekends, with the endless procession of school projects, sporting events, and other functions. Their Lifestyle Balance Analysis confirmed that they lived a "red-shoe existence," a term I coined from the fairy tale about a girl who donned red shoes and couldn't stop dancing. Anne, Henry, and the kids were all wearing bright red shoes and were dancing way too fast to be happy.

Their home was unsurprisingly dominated by Yang features that anchored their overly active lifestyle in place. Yang households often look like they've been "hit by a tornado," as there's precious little time allotted to maintaining order. There are too many people to see, places to go, and things to do! No one has an extra minute to sort the mail, do the laundry, organize the pantry, prepare a home-cooked meal, or put things back where they belong. Every room in Anne and Henry's home was appointed with a chaotic array of papers, toys, and clothes spun in among the furniture.

And it was all glaringly bright. During the day, light poured in through the many windows, some of which had neither shades nor curtains. At night, fluorescent bulbs blazed in the kitchen, laundry room, bathrooms, and master closet. The living, family, and dining rooms were glaringly lit, while several standing lamps shot the ceilings with more light. The dining room was doubled in size and brightness by a large mirrored wall, and the kids' neon-bright, action-themed bedrooms were brightly reflected in mirrored closet doors. The master bedroom, located in the Love and Marriage area of their home's Bagua Map (Appendix A) was strictly functional and lacked any sensuality. The television across from the bed and the exercise bike next to it spoke loudly of more activity.

Other Yang features dominated the architecture and decor of the house, with large white rooms, high ceilings and windows in the living and dining areas, and oversized furniture. There was a decided lack of pillows, artwork, and other embellishments that soften, personalize, and beautify a home. The few attempts to add Yin elements were in sad shape. Houseplants drooped from lack of water in various parts of the house. A fruit bowl sat on the kitchen counter holding one black banana and a withered apple. Next to the sink was a bouquet of dead flowers jammed into a jar. Here, the effort to bring a nurturing quality into the house fell far short of the mark. Henry and Anne's wish for some serene moments and romantic interludes simply ricocheted off the bright white walls and went out the door. There wasn't a single place in the house that invited them to kick back, relax, and enjoy some intimate moments together.

Sound the harp and usher in Madam Yin! Without her, Master Yang was in a complete frenzy, taking the family who lived there with him. The following recommendations were made to balance the family's home and lifestyle:

Top priority: Turn the bedrooms into retreats for each family member:

1. Encourage the children to sleep peacefully each night by curtaining the mirrored closet doors like large windows, and drawing the curtains closed at night. Replace neon colors and action-figure themes with calming and cuddly "teddy-bear" colors such as beige, cocoa brown, peach, mauve, raspberry, gold, pale yellow, lavender, terra-cotta, or burgundy. Put a covered wicker "treasure" chest in each of their rooms for toy storage.

2. Teddy-bear colors also describe the many welcoming shades for the master bedroom. Think of pastel and darker colors that come from skin tones. Choose your favorites for wall color, high-quality natural fiber linens, and other types of decor, and wrap the bedroom in them. Think "sumptuous, sensual, and romantic" when making your choices, as your bedroom is your special retreat and holds the space for Love and Marriage.

3. Relocate the exercise bike and add lounge furniture, such as two comfortable chairs or a small couch. Include a small table and a lamp that can be used for reading or creating a romantic atmosphere.

4. Remove the television from your bedroom, or place it in a covered cabinet or armoire.

These suggestions focus on the rest of the house:

5. Install rheostats (dimmers) on all light switches throughout the house so that lighting can be adjusted to create a variety of atmospheres.

6. Install fitted shades and/or curtains on the windows.

7. Create a reading nook in the living room with two comfortable chairs. Make a point of enjoying some quiet time there on a daily basis.

8. Put the family-room television and stereo equipment in a cabinet, and keep the doors closed when not in use.

9. Move the dining-room sideboard to the mirrored wall to diminish the size of the mirror and "calm" the room down. Decorate the sideboard with items that are beautifully reflected in the mirror, such as candles and flowers or a favorite platter, bowl, or tray. Consider having a candlelit dinner with the family and/or friends in the dining room at least once a week.

10. Keep your plants vibrantly healthy throughout the house. Replace them with silk if you don't wish to maintain living plants.

11. Replenish the kitchen fruit bowl with fresh fruit each week as a symbol of the family's health and vitality.

12. Embellish the house with items that make you feel good whenever you see them. Plants, fruit, flowers, candles, pillows, and art are just a few examples. Choose things that elicit happiness and don't require more care than you enjoy giving.

13. Establish a family habit of daily "pick-ups" around the house. Create simple systems that make the job easier and more fun, such as placing easy-to-use storage baskets and trunks in each bedroom.

Anne and Henry got started immediately. They painted their bedroom a golden camel tone and dressed their bed in luxurious caramel and deep cranberry cotton linens. They sold the exercise bicycle (it had been used exactly once), replaced it with a comfortable love seat, and bought an armoire for the television. The room took on a sensual atmosphere that was very inviting, and they began to snuggle in bed at night and watch movies after the kids were asleep.

"We'd never done that before," Anne told me. "We always avoided our bedroom until we were dead tired at night. Now it's become our private retreat, and we spend a lot of evening time there."

They also involved the children in redecorating their rooms. Their daughter, Lisa, chose pale lilac, peach, and mint-green floral linens and a lilac wall color, a vast departure from the busy neon blue and yellow decor she'd had before. Anne had curtains made from the same soft floral material and hung them over Lisa's mirrored closet doors. Her room took on the feeling of a peaceful garden.

Derek, their son, immediately gravitated to cocoa-brown flannel linens, having taken the teddy-bear color suggestion quite literally. Pale apricot walls and a new display shelf of favorite stuffed animals tucked him into a bedroom that had been previously aflame with bright red action figures.

"They're different children," Henry said. "They've both settled down and aren't so frenetic. At first, we held our breath and waited for the spell to be broken. But they really have calmed down!"

The spell Henry is referring to is the balanced atmosphere in their home. Children often have remarkably positive responses when Yin and Yang influences are just right. But then, so do adults. Over the next couple of months, Anne and Henry made the rest of the suggested changes. Their lifestyle remains active, with one very big difference. It's now balanced and "softened around the edges" with relaxing times. All through the house there are places to calm down, read, daydream, and essentially engage in Yin pastimes.

Anne and Henry are enjoying a delicious renewal of romance in their marriage, and both children are thriving. "It reminds me of that saying from *Field of Dreams:* 'If you build it, they will come,'" Anne said. "We 'built' places throughout the house that are very inviting to spend time in. We eat dinner together frequently, which we almost never did before. It's pretty miraculous!" Anne's sense of the miraculous is her experience of balance. She's learned to bring the dance of heart and home into the everyday rhythm of her family's life.

PART II

ROMANCING THE HOME, ROOM BY ROOM

IN FENG SHUI, every square inch of your home is considered equal in importance. It all counts. To hold happiness in place, it's important to balance the whole house with just the right amount of Yin and Yang influences. Let's take a walk through your domain and focus on bringing the balance that best serves you into each area.

Chapter 4

The Front Entrance

—

Welcoming Happiness into Your Home

THE AREA LEADING up to your front door, the door itself, and the foyer area immediately inside set the mood for your entire house. This is the "face" of your home, where first impressions are made, and where *you*, your friends, and community register immediate and lasting feelings about who you are. If happiness is what you wish for, this is your first stop. This is the threshold where romancing your home begins, where the gracious essence of Madam Yin greets the worldly Master Yang and welcomes him in. The more entrancing this area, the better, as it's the magnetic gateway through which you attract heavenly opportunities and good fortune into your home. When openly welcoming, it draws the best that life has to offer to your door.

For those who live in apartments or places where embellishing the outside of the front entrance isn't safe or possible, simply focus on making the foyer area just inside the front door as welcoming as it can possibly be.

OUTSIDE:

1. Include pleasant, safety-conscious lighting and a meandering pathway to the front door. A path that's wide enough (four feet or more) to allow two people to approach side by side is ideal.

2. Keep the pathway clear of anything that hinders clear passage. This includes overgrown foliage and any possessions that obstruct the full use of the path.

3. An attractive gate, arbor, bridge, or fountain can add interest and beauty to your front entrance design. Other special touches include outdoor seating, garden walls, statuary, nature objects, interesting plants, wreaths, and chimes.

4. Consider making your front door a beautiful point of focus. Red, the traditional color of celebration in Feng Shui, is a popular choice in door color and can be captured in the many tones of crimson, terra-cotta, burgundy, purple, or magenta. If these colors aren't your favorites, any color you love is a good choice. Or choose a door that's beautifully made or has an artistic appeal.

INSIDE:

1. To enhance your sense of comfort and safety, you should be able to see who's knocking at the door before you open it. Ideally, you can see through a peephole or window, but your visitor cannot see into the house until you've opened the door. Install curtains or shades on front doors made primarily of glass to assure privacy.

2. Let your foyer area offer a warm embrace to all who enter your home. Even the smallest of spaces can be adorned with a favorite painting, mirror, or other "greeter" that symbolizes a welcoming reception. In larger foyers, an aquarium, carved statue, or arrangements of furniture, plants, and lighting can enhance the space.

3. Be careful not to overcrowd the foyer in an effort to make it welcoming. Remove anything that blocks the full swing of front or closet doors, and keep the area clear of migrating possessions such as toys, sports equipment, recyclables, and mail.

4. Whatever room you see first when entering your front door tends to set the focus for the entire house. A view directly into the living or other public room is ideal, whereas a view into a bedroom or bathroom is considered too personal for first impressions. An immediate view into the kitchen or dining room can put too much emphasis on "what's to eat." To change a questionable or unsightly view, creatively rearrange furniture, close doors, or add screens or curtains to better define the foyer area.

5. If multiple rooms can be seen from the foyer, highlight one room by defining a clear path to it. Brightly lighting one room and leaving another dimly lit is a sure way to lead people "toward the light." Screens or plants placed to mark a path will subtly direct people into the desired room.

6. Often considered "insignificant," a secondary entrance through a laundry room, back hall, mudroom, or garage is quite important, as it often ushers you out into the world and welcomes you home again. Make it bright, inviting, and completely accessible. Display fun photos, collages,

and personal mementos that might not fit in other areas of the house. Or, beautify a secondary entrance with a splash of finery such as an oil painting or gilt-framed mirror. Whatever you choose, enhance it to lift your spirits and offer a warm welcome home.

Chapter 5

THE LIVING ROOM

—

SHOWING THE WORLD WHO YOU ARE

THE LIVING ROOM
is well placed as the
first room you enter from
the foyer. Because it's primarily
Master Yang's domain as a socially
active room, the living room is the
perfect place to "put yourself out
there" and show the world who you
are through the art, colors, and collections you display. Simultaneously, a more
Yin atmosphere can be only a dimmer
switch away to bring out the romantic
quality of the room. Here, the focus is
to creatively express your individuality
in the design style that suits you,
while arranging your furnishings
and treasures to please all of
your senses.

1. "Romance" the living room by making it as safe and comfortable as possible. The Yin influence guides you in choosing seating that embraces you in deep comfort, while the safety-focused Yang force arranges the primary seating (usually a couch) with a full or peripheral view of the door. When this isn't possible, a mirror can be strategically placed to capture a view of the door from that seating. To further refine the balance of the living room and enhance its comfort quotient, also give the other living room seating a full, partial, or mirror view of the door.

2. Check the view from every seat in the living room, and correct any eyesores. Remove any clutter, and appoint corners with beauty marks like plants, lighting, and furniture.

3. Choose furnishings with friendly detailing and rounded corners. Camouflage existing sharp corners or unsafe detailing with tablecloths, plants, and other decor, or place them out of harm's way.

4. The fireplace, an archetypal symbol of romance, can really add atmosphere to the living room. Make sure that it is indeed a beautiful focal point where a fire is always laid or candles are ready to be lit. Or, screen the fireplace opening and appoint the area around it according to mood and season.

5. Finding the right balance of decorative items in the living room depends a great deal on your style and needs. Be sure your decorations carry strong positive associations, and distinctly add to the feeling you wish to convey in the room.

6. Collections grow over time. If you're intimate with Madam Yin, you have a love for ornamentation. This love is reflected in collections of art, pillows, containers, and other house

jewelry that become too large for the living room to "wear" all at one time. Accessorize your living room as you would your clothing. Choose a select few items to display, store the rest where you can easily get to them, and change the look whenever the mood strikes. This refreshes the living room and encourages expression of your "latest self." Cull your collections often, and keep only those things that are filled with positive memories and associations.

7. Locate televisions and other electronic equipment in an armoire or cabinets that conceal them when not in use. This one simple adjustment can dramatically improve the romantic quality of life by promoting a variety of other activities, including quiet conversation and intimacy. When watching television or listening to music, be aware of the quality of your choices. The more active, upbeat, or thrilling the programming, the more Yang it is, while Yin selections are more peaceful and relaxing.

8. When you'd like to slow down the active Yang focus of a living room, light candles, play soft music, serve special foods on beautiful dishes, and group furniture together for intimate conversation.

Chapter 6

The Dining Room

—

Relishing the Good Life

THE DINING ROOM
holds enormous romantic potential. It's one of the portals through which Madam Yin can bring more serenity into an all-too-frenetic lifestyle. Taking pleasure in dining on a regular basis is a significant lifestyle choice that underlies a commitment to balance. By slowing down enough to really dine, you invite a romantic quality to become part of your daily routine, one that transforms the act of grabbing a bite into a meaningful ritual that provides even greater sustenance. Dining alone in a delicious atmosphere is an act of self-love, while sharing a meal with others provides conversation and companionship that's as nurturing to the heart and spirit as it is to the body. The more hectic your days are, the more important this ritual is to your overall balance.

1. Make it a point to create an atmosphere that's truly relaxing—a place that has its own intimate, peaceful atmosphere. Arrange furniture, plants, and area rugs to define and beautify a dining space that supports reflection, digestion, and intimate conversation. Honor your senses by inviting your favorite colors, textures, scents, sounds, and tastes to be frequent "guests" at your table. Turn off the phone, light candles, play soft music, and include flowers, table linens, and other enhancements that enrich your dining experience.

2. Put all your lighting on dimmer switches to create the perfect dining atmosphere.

3. Because comfort is so important in Feng Shui, ergonomics—the study of the human body's physiostructural needs—is always considered. Dining chairs pass the safety and comfort test when they're form-fitting, with cushioned or upholstered seats and backs that embrace the contours of your body. Just like shoes, dining chairs that are both comfortable and beautiful strike the perfect balance.

4. Sit before buying! No matter how perfect a chair looks in a brochure or catalog, it's not a sure thing until you actually take a seat. When choosing your dining furniture, select chairs that all offer the same level of comfort. This promotes good conversation and a comforting sense of equality around the table.

5. Check the view from every chair. Remove clutter and other eyesores, embellish views with beautiful things, and screen (or don't illuminate) unsightly views, such as those that might look directly into a messy kitchen.

6. Feng Shui favors simple round and oval dining-table designs without lurking underbraces or sharp detailing. If you prefer a rectangular table, choose one with rounded edges and corners, or drape those with sharp corners.

7. Ideally, the size of your dining table matches your needs. A "table for two" is best for a couple's daily use, while a family needs a larger table. A large table can be made to feel more intimate by setting one section for dining, and

appointing the rest of the surface with "eye candy" such as flowers, fruit, art objects, and candles.

8. If you have no official place to dine in your home, now is the time to create one. Please let go of the habit of dining in front of the television! Although occasionally fun, this habit can rob you of the precious time you have to be in quiet reflection or conversation with loved ones.

9. Ceiling fans are a necessity in some climates, but they can pose a Feng Shui challenge. When hung directly over dining tables, their blades can appear too close for comfort and cause a decided lack of serenity at the table. If a ceiling fan is a must in the dining room, choose a neutral-colored simple design and hang it as high as possible above or away from the table.

10. The dining room is a place for art with a serene, nurturing quality. Pictures of fruit or flowers are good choices, as well as landscapes, waterscapes, and art depicting people enjoying calm and leisurely pastimes. Avoid pieces

that are disturbing or overpowering in color or content. A large mirror that reflects the diners can overactivate the space and hurry them through their meal. (Notice the many restaurants that use bright colors, busy art, and large mirrors to discourage patrons from lingering at the table.) Relocate the mirror if you can, or reduce its size by placing a sideboard or other decorative furniture in front of it.

Chapter 7

The Kitchen

—

Nurturing Your Body, Heart, and Spirit

EVER NOTICE HOW your friends and family love to congregate in the kitchen? Often considered the heart of the home, the kitchen has a magical quality that we're instinctively attracted to. Here, a cornucopia of ingredients transform into life-sustaining repasts. This is territory equally shared by Madam Yin and Master Yang. Her influence organizes the pantry, muses over recipes, and patiently chops ingredients, while his enthusiasm and creativity bursts forth in the active preparation of a delicious meal.

To cook is to display a full range of talent, as you must be impeccably organized and also wildly creative simultaneously. Here, more than in any other room in the house, you see the daily dance of

Yin and Yang as you make a royal mess . . . and then clean it up. Let your kitchen come alive with the alchemical delight of creative food preparation, as it strengthens the balance of Yin and Yang and enriches heart and home.

1. Enhance the ambience in your kitchen by celebrating the bounty of Nature. Display bowls of fresh fruit and vegetables, plates of baked goods, braids of garlic and peppers, pots of growing herbs, or vases of flowers.

2. Invite Madam Yin's boundless capacity to organize space into your kitchen. Take a look at what lives on your counters and remove little-used appliances and gadgets that clutter your workspace. Claim your kitchen countertops for the things you use often, and put everything else away! This creates the ideal conditions in which to relax and enjoy meal preparation.

3. As you clear the clutter from counters, you'll probably encounter crowded cabinets, drawers, and pantries. Remove excess jars, plastic containers, appliances, dishes,

and dry goods so that you have plenty of room to organize the things you do need in your kitchen. (See Chapter 12, Storage Areas, for more organizing tips.)

4. Store trash and recycling containers out of sight. In most kitchens, the cabinets or pantry can be organized to accommodate trash containers so that they remain convenient but hidden. When this isn't possible, be sure to choose attractive trash receptacles with lids.

5. When you have the chance, design kitchen countertops to curve or have rounded corners, knowing that such designs encourage a safer, happier dance around the kitchen.

6. Knives, although necessary in the kitchen, can be dangerous and are instinctually viewed as weapons. Your kitchen will feel safer and more peaceful when you store knives and other sharp blades out of sight.

7. Overhead hanging racks, when suspended over work areas, can be a hazard. For safety's sake, use a wall rack when you don't have enough cabinets to store your kitchenware.

8. The stove, with its heat and power to transform raw ingredients into something delectable, is quite Yang. It's ideal to have a commanding view from the stove, one from which you can easily see the entryway into the kitchen. If no such view is available from your stove, capture one in a mirror, shiny metal tray, or other reflective surface strategically located behind or beside the stove. A stove is well placed on an island, as it empowers the cook with a good view and centralizes food preparation.

9. Keep your stove clean and use all the burners regularly, thus symbolizing the abundant circulation of vital energy in your life.

10. Seating is an environmental embrace. Every kitchen needs perches that invite family and guests to gather and stay

awhile. If your kitchen doesn't provide space for a table and chairs, place a stool or two in a corner, or locate chairs nearby that can easily be brought in when needed.

11. Cooking and food preparation require good lighting, but preferably not from fluorescent lights! You'll make the kitchen a much more inviting and appealing place to be by replacing fluorescent lights with incandescent or halogen lighting. When this isn't possible, use full-spectrum fluorescent bulbs.

Chapter 8

THE HOME OFFICE

—

SITTING ON TOP OF THE WORLD

WITH A CONSTANT focus on creative pro-ductivity, the home office is your place of personal power. Because it's often quite Yang in ori-entation, it can easily slip into a chaotic state. Here you must encourage the happy union between Madam Yin and Master Yang by establishing systems that keep your work activities organized. While the Yang creative force only wishes to move projects forward quickly and expand to new horizons of wealth and success, Yin quietly institutes the systems that keep the home office humming smoothly along. The saying, "Behind every successful man is a woman" takes on a whole new meaning as all of us, men and women alike, learn that our success depends on being organized.

1. Ideally, when your work is actively people oriented—that is, related to sales and service—your home office is located in the front of the house or where Yang-oriented rooms are usually found. The more Yin-oriented rooms in the back of the house are best suited for art, writing, and other inwardly focused vocations. (See Chapter 10, The Sanctuary.)

2. No matter what type of work you do, you'll benefit from good desk or worktable placement. The ideal position is where you have a direct or peripheral view of the door from your chair, a pleasant view out a window, and a solid wall behind you. The supportive Yin embrace from behind and commanding Yang view from the front places you in the power position and promotes success in your work. A strategically placed mirror can afford a better view for built-in or cubicle desks, while inspiring art and other enhancements can be arranged to give a pleasing view. When you must have a

window behind you, place plants or furniture between your chair and the window to promote a sense of support and stability.

3. Claiming the power position in your home office often means positioning your desk or worktable like an island in the room, rather than pushing it against a wall. It's best when electrical outlets are in the middle of the floor so that you won't have to run wires over to a wall. Or, enclose unsightly wires in a tube designed to hold them (available at any office-supply store) or camouflage them behind plants, screens, or under area rugs.

4. Keep stress and irritability to a minimum by choosing furniture with rounded corners. Position items with sharp corners out of the traffic flow by turning them at a diagonal in the room or storing them in closets.

5. Ignite your creativity and sense of prosperity by choosing office components that really suit your needs. For instance, you may need more than one desk or working surface in

the room to flourish. You may find that the addition of a couch or conference table adds to your comfort and supports your ability to effectively get the job done. This is the room that houses your productivity, efficiency, and creativity, so be diligent in meeting all of your needs as closely as possible.

6. Regard your chair as a regal piece of office equipment, and choose it well. Your capacity to produce and prosper is considerably enhanced by a great work chair. Treat yourself to an ergonomically correct chair that has excellent lumbar support and adjustable height. Most people thrive in a chair that rocks back and forth, has sturdy casters, a high back, a headrest, and adjustable armrests. Always sit in a chair before you buy it—that's the only way to know if you've truly found your throne.

7. The electromagnetic field (EMF) of electrical equipment is often an issue in a home office. An electromagnetic field tester can give you an idea of the EMF you're exposed to when you use your computer, fax machine, and other electronic equipment. Your best defense is to know what level of EMF your equipment generates, and then to stay out of range when they're on, usually a minimum of three feet.

8. Productivity isn't long lived without the Yin influence of organization. To get organized takes time—time that could always be spent in so many other ways. Unite your Yin and Yang energies and become the "samurai of clutter" (see Chapter 12, Storage Areas). Your ability to attract new opportunities depends on your spending a few Yin minutes a day returning things to order, or chaos will inevitably reign. If you find yourself buried in chaos and can't seem to pull yourself out, hire a Feng Shui practitioner with professional organizing expertise to identify your personal work style and help you organize your workspace.

A little romance belongs in every room. Ideally, your home office draws you in like a bee to honey. Remove blah art and mismatched furniture and paint at least one wall a WOW! color. Make it "unusually" attractive by including the sights, sounds, scents, and materials that inspire and empower your creative genius.

Chapter 9

The Bedroom

—

Claiming Your Oasis of Serenity and Sensuality

SERENITY AND SEN-suality—two key characteristics of a happy existence—tence—are currently endangered in our Western culture. Their main habitat: the bedroom. This is primarily Madam Yin's domain, a room meant for sleeping, dreaming, romancing, and recharging your batteries—the perfect antidotes to a busy day. However, with an all-consuming interest in activity, many bedrooms have become just as busy as the rest of the house. All too often, for children and adults alike, they function more as home offices, media rooms, or exercise studios with a bed thrown in somewhere. This kind of arrangement eliminates the soothing ministrations of Madam Yin and can cause many imbalances including sleep disorders and chronic exhaustion.

When this last refuge is stripped away, you have no place to go to really relax and be nurtured in a soothing Yin atmosphere. The more active and "crazy" your lifestyle, the more crucial it is to reinstate balance by claiming your bedroom as an oasis of rest, rejuvenation, and romance. Make the bedroom so sensually attractive and comfortable that you melt into "her" warm embrace every night, sleep well, have sweet dreams, and awaken refreshed and energized.

1. Return the bedroom to its original role, and appoint your bed as the king or queen of the room. Chaise longues and overstuffed chairs add to the restful atmosphere, while desks, computers, televisions, and exercise equipment drop-kick sensuality and serenity out of the room. Just when you're ready to call it a night, these "busy-bodies" proclaim that there are bills, e-mails, news programs, and flabby body parts that need immediate attention. When they must share the bedroom with you, maintain serenity by covering them or screening them from the bed.

2. To honor your instinctual need for comfort and safety, place your bed so that you can easily get to both sides and see

the bedroom entrance without being directly in front of it. When your bed must be located directly in front of the door, a footboard or trunk can suggest protection between you and the door. If there's a window directly overhead, add a headboard and window treatments to shelter you from direct exposure and promote the feeling of safety.

3. Nightstands and lighting on both sides of the bed symbolize equality in a relationship and help to hold happiness in place. Choose nightstand designs that are in scale with your bedroom so that both partners are accommodated.

4. If you're single and would like to be partnered, act as if the love of your life has already arrived by moving the bed away from the wall and giving your "one night stand" a partner. You don't want to hold your singleness in place by having a bedroom that comfortably accommodates only one! Clear the bed of delicate "guardians," such as lacy pillows and stuffed animals, and update with enhancements that accurately reflect your current romantic intentions. Remove pictures of solitary people or things; and

arrange decorations in pairs, like two flowers, candles, or poetry books. Design an approachable, sensuous bedroom that invites a partner to join you without a "single" care.

5. For safety's sake, hang only lightweight or solidly anchored items over the bed. Check for sharp corners or protruding designs on nightstands, bed frames, and other furniture that may pose danger to sleepy—or amorous—body parts. If you can't replace such furniture, wrap, drape, or skirt it as needed to enhance the relaxed feeling in the room.

6. Seen every morning and night, your view from the bed influences your view of the world. Make it a fabulous one! Improve a view that goes directly into a bathroom by curtaining or screening the threshold between the two rooms. Close closet doors, and create an inspiring view with sensual art, restful colors, and other special elements. Remove photos and other items that compromise your sense of privacy by appearing to watch you in bed. Relocate family photos to more public areas of the house, or to children's bedrooms where they provide a sense of security and connection.

7. Mirrors promote the wakeful Yang qualities of any room by enhancing the size and brightness of the space. In the bedroom, the bigger a mirror is, and the closer it is to the bed, the more likely that it will disturb your sleep. Because it's often impractical or undesirable to remove large mirrors such as mirrored closet doors, consider curtaining them like a window. This gives you the flexibility of "opening" the mirror during the day and "closing" it at night. You can also drape bureau mirrors and other smaller ones with beautiful cloths to calm the bedroom's atmosphere at night.

8. Assess the memories and feelings that are being held in place by the things in your bedroom. As with every room in the house, it's best when everything in your bedroom has pleasantly nurturing associations. When you let go of any object that triggers negative feelings, thoughts, or memories, you change the atmosphere to one that's conducive to rest and relaxation.

9. You are as connected to what's behind closet doors and drawers as you are to the things that are in plain sight in your home. It all counts. Cluttered, disorganized closets and bureaus are the result of an overly Yang lifestyle and cause daily confusion, overwhelm, irritation, and other mood "inflammations." (See Chapter 12, Storage Areas.) Order in the bedroom allows for complete relaxation and promotes happiness, clarity, and personal power in your daily life.

10. Clear any clutter from under the bed, and keep it clean and airy. If you absolutely must store items beneath the bed, keep them neat and handsomely corralled in containers made for under-the-bed storage.

11. Consider how often you "wear" your bed linens and splurge on the best, knowing that you spend about a third of your life wrapped up in them! Choose the sensual embrace of high-thread-count natural fabrics including flannel, silk, and cotton. Look for colors that are found in the skin tones of people around the world—beige, pink,

peach, yellow, and caramel, as well as the more pig-mented tones of coral, lavender, terra-cotta, cinnabar, raspberry, violet, burgundy, chocolate, gold, and bronze. Pure white, gray, black, blues, and gray-greens work as accents, but too much of them can take away from the coziness of a bedroom. When cool tones dominate, bring in complementary warm tones via wall color, linens, accent pillows, art, slipcovers, area rugs, tablecloths, flow-ers, and candles. And, as always, choose only what turns you on!

12. You can benefit from sleeping with your head facing north, south, east, or west, depending on your needs. In general, when your head is pointing north, your physical health and vitality are strengthened. South enhances intu-ition and can stimulate dream and memory recall, west is calming and helps remedy restlessness or insomnia, and east is revitalizing, relieving sluggishness and depression. Sleeping northwest, northeast, southwest, or southeast blends the qualities of the two primary directions.

13. Children also need a serene bedroom environment. It's very common to find children's bedroom decor to be neon bright, very busy, and overstimulating. All of the above suggestions will also tuck your children into the tranquil embrace of a cozy, serene bedroom where they can calm down and get the rest they need.

14. While every room in the house should have a sensual appeal, let the bedroom glow with your personal mark of sensuality. It's your private domain, an oasis of pleasure, and the place to celebrate your senses. Create an enchanting atmosphere with scented candles or oils, soothing music, amorous colors, and seductive fabrics. When you take your restful and romantic interludes as seriously as you do your work activities, you're allowing the Yin and Yang influences to balance and enhance your life. Give your senses the lead, and enjoy being sensually delighted every night.

Chapter 10

The Sanctuary

—

Rejuvenating Your Spirit

WHEREAS a bedroom is dedicated to the total rejuvenation of your body, the sanctuary is devoted to spirit. It's a room or a place dedicated to the exploration of your soul's passions and interests. It may be a completely quiet and peacefully Yin space assigned to the practice of yoga, healing, or meditation, or it may take the more actively creative Yang form of an art or dance studio. A sanctuary is a sure sign of self-love, as it reflects a fervent desire to explore the soulful depths of life.

Perhaps you've blended your soul's expression with your career path to the degree that your sanctuary and home office can share the same space. Both are "hybrid" spaces and have only recently been designed into some new homes.

Fortunately, just about any room or place—including a guest room, den, spare room, basement, attic, garage, or library—can be outfitted to specifically meet your needs.

1. When a sanctuary is dedicated to introspective Yin pastimes, deepen the atmosphere with soft lighting; low furnishings; and dark, restful colors. Madam Yin loves the layered look, so consider installing ornate window treatments, laying area rugs over carpeting, or grouping plush pillows and plants around the room. Choose a special spot where you can arrange candles, incense, flowers, and inspiring icons, pictures, and books to anchor your soulful life into place.

2. In sanctuaries designed for more Yang activity, accentuate the setting with an abundance of natural light, bright or pastel colors, and space! Master Yang loves room to move, so leave the floors as open and unadorned as possible, with minimal furniture for maximum movement. Choose clean, plain furniture designs that are modular, or add casters so they can be moved around with relative ease. Large mirrors and flashy bigger-than-life focal points are perfect here. Think big, bold, and beautiful!

3. A sanctuary can be created in a corner or alcove of just about any room. Many people create a small space in their bedrooms where they light a candle and sit quietly each day. There are artists who keep an easel and paints in an alcove for when the mood strikes. We find sanctuary where we can. If you haven't already done so, claim a space that's purposely dedicated to your soul's desire for growth, connection, and expression.

4. Couples and families are usually happiest when every family member has a sanctuary space to call their own. When each person's needs are met in this way, compromising on the design and arrangement of shared areas usually becomes a much easier process.

Chapter 11

The Bathroom

Enjoying Your Everyday Spa

MADAM Yin would like to set something straight, once and for all. Bathrooms are *good!* Just imagine your life without them—not a pretty picture. Which is precisely the problem. Most bathrooms aren't pretty pictures, and any room that's an eyesore is a drain on habitat and inhabitants alike. Bathrooms also contain the piece of plumbing that has the biggest opening in the house—the toilet. When the lid—or worse, the seat and the lid—are left open, the eye is drawn there. And where the eye goes, the vital energy goes—in this case, down the drain.

In Feng Shui, our goal is to lift the eye up into a buoyant and beautiful space that maintains the vitality of heart and home. This is quite possible to do in a bathroom.

In fact, it can be one of the easiest and most affordable rooms to transform in the house. Take Madam Yin's lead, and make it a relaxing, soothing, and sensual place to be.

1. Begin by keeping the toilet lid shut. For many people, this takes training, but it's worth it. Notice where your eye goes when the lid is open, and where it goes when the toilet is shut, and you'll literally see what a difference it makes. If sink or bath drains draw your eye, pull the stoppers closed, or cover them with small rubber mats made for that purpose.

2. When all else fails in homes with young children and boys "still in training," keep the bathroom door closed. This is made easier by installing a soft spring on the door so that it opens easily and closes softly behind you. Even when the toilet lid is open, choose an extra-fabulous piece of art or other eye-catching enhancements to draw the eye up, up, and away from the open plumbing.

3. When designing a bathroom, place the toilet so that you don't see it from the bathroom door. Locate it in its own "water closet" or behind a wall or screen. And even when it's nicely tucked away, keep the lid closed.

4. Make all bathrooms wonderful places to visit! You can rejuvenate the saddest little bathroom with a fresh coat of paint, new bathroom linens, candles, art, scented soaps, plants, and lighting.

5. If your bedroom is directly connected to a bathroom without a door, make it a priority to install a door, curtain, or screen to visually separate the bathroom from the bedroom. This assures privacy, adds visual serenity, and enhances the romantic atmosphere of the bedroom.

6. To transform the mood of a bathroom, put the lights on a dimmer and/or add a low-wattage lamp. This ensures that a romantic spa atmosphere is only a flick of a switch away.

7. Small bathrooms appear larger and more welcoming when you add art that has depth. Art hung directly across from a mirror repeats the view of the art and enriches the bathroom's ambience. Avoid hanging two mirrors directly across from each other, as the resultant view into infinity distorts the space.

8. Preserve the bathroom's serenity by keeping the counters, bath area, and cabinets free of clutter. Enjoy your cosmetics down to the last drop, and then let the bottles go! Enlist the help of baskets and trays to keep bathroom necessities organized.

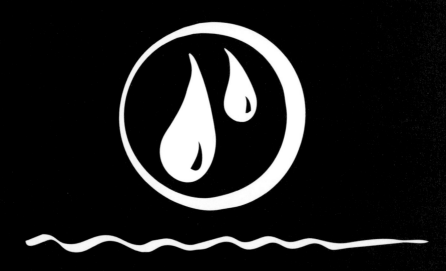

Chapter 12

STORAGE AREAS

—

GIVING EVERYTHING A GOOD HOME

HAVE YOU EVER had the experience of stepping into a completely organized closet, garage, basement, or attic; or opening a cabinet or drawer to find everything in its place? I'd never had the pleasure until I met my husband, Brian, whose military background gave him all the necessary skills to keep his environment organized. His secret: a few minutes a day. In that brief amount of time, he slows down, embraces Madam Yin, and attends to the things that the day's activities have whirled out of place. He systematically moves through his home office and the rest of the house, putting the puzzle back together again like clockwork.

Along with learning a whole new strategy for staying organized, I'm fascinated by what Brian is demonstrating. By and large, he's a very outgoing, active, Yang person, and his Yin organizational skills came from a remarkably Yang institution—the Navy. Here, I see the no-nonsense approach to "what works." What works is balance. Forget the mysterious Eastern terminology. The speed and force of the navy is compromised if it's not *very* organized, down to the last detail, and this is true for all of us. Yang cannot do a proper job without the "re-storing" energy of Yin by his side. Their connection, their embrace, their dance, is what makes your life work well. Brian and his navy buddies may not put it that way, but they are handsome examples of the elegant dance of Yin and Yang.

The "Few Minutes a Day" technique works best once order has been established, so put "Restore Order Now" at the top of your priority list. Your storage areas are as important as the most lived-in areas of your household. As you know, everything counts, including what's found behind closed doors! The more Yang your lifestyle, the more important it is to take a few minutes a day to restore order. Without the balance of this Yin time, your possessions, your energy level, and your quality of life can quickly spin out of control.

From Chaos City to Personal Paradise

There are three gateways into Chaos City, and they're easy to identify. They exist wherever you enter into a state of *Confusion*, *Irritation*, or *Overwhelm* when trying to find something. These gateways are most often found in storage areas—the garage, basement, attic, storeroom, closets, cabinets, and drawers.

Organizing possessions and eliminating clutter can be viewed as an adventurous mission, where against all odds you seal the gateways into Chaos City and open the portals into your Personal Paradise. You'll know you've succeeded in reinstating balance when you respond positively to every part of your home, and can *easily* put your hands on anything you need, at any time.

1. Let the active Yang force take the lead by filling the space to be organized with bright light and upbeat music you really enjoy (rock 'n' roll moves many people through their organizing projects). And plan to do something special after you've completed the job, knowing that you're celebrating an inspiring change in your life.

2. Take the time to "get Yin" and group like items together so that you can see what you've got. As you do this, ask:

   ♥ Do I love it?

   ♥ Do I need it?

   ♥ Does it represent and support who I am now?

   ♥ What pleasant or unpleasant memories or associations does it hold in place for me, and do I wish to continue to share my home with it?

   ♥ Do I own duplicates of items that I can let go of now?

   ♥ Does it need repair, and am I willing to restore it to its best condition now?

♥ If I'm letting it go, will I sell, lend, or give it away, and when? (The sooner, the better!)

3. This sorting process can be one of the most challenging parts of your task, as this is the stuff that's holding confusion, overwhelm, and irritation in place. Be patient with the process so that you become very clear why you're keeping every item. Let go of the rest immediately by giving it away, taking it to a charity or resale shop, or putting in an area awaiting imminent pickup!

4. Give yourself the gift of all the shelves, cabinets, and containers you need to organize what you're keeping. Remember, everything deserves a good home. Group like items together, such as garden tools, sports equipment, hobby supplies, and memorabilia. Consider arranging the same types of clothing together in closets—such as blouses, jackets, slacks, and accessories. Follow the same "likes attract" strategy in bedroom drawers, kitchen cabinets, and linen closets. Storage areas don't have to be fancy (although Madam Yin is most satisfied when storage

furniture and containers are both attractive and functional); they just need to be organized so that you can easily find what you're looking for.

5. Many people's garages are sprawling Chaos Cities that have taken over the space meant for their automobiles. When organizing your garage, assess whether the things stored there are worth more than your car. In almost every case, they're not, so give your car top priority, move it back inside, and organize around it.

6. If necessary, rent a storage locker for precious items that take too much space in your current storage areas. And when friends and family members wish to store their things in your storage areas, invite them to rent a locker, too!

7. Storage areas, large and small, are spread throughout your home, so be creative and embellish them to enhance their personality. As with secondary entrances, you can brighten them up with things that beautify the space. Keeping your

storage areas organized becomes easier when they're fun, interesting places in which to spend time.

Your environment displays your consciousness, and there's no more revealing place to look than in your storage areas. By getting rid of the things you no longer want or need, you revitalize your home and make room for what you really *do* want to flow into your life. When you make your storage areas pleasant and organized—with every possession well cared for—you enhance the happiness, clarity, and peace of mind that defines your Personal Paradise.

How to Use the CD

The CD included with this book is a Feng Shui meditation that takes you on an inner journey through your home. It's meant to deepen your experience of your personal environment, heighten gratitude, and promote positive change.

It's important that you listen to the CD while sitting or lying down in a quiet, relaxing Yin atmosphere. You can do this alone or with a small group of family or friends. Sharing your experiences of the meditation with others can provide wonderful insights, clarify decorating decisions, and generate creative solutions to design challenges.

Please refrain from listening to this CD while driving a car or doing any other Yang-oriented activity.

Appendix A

When Desire and Structure Become One: The Bagua Map

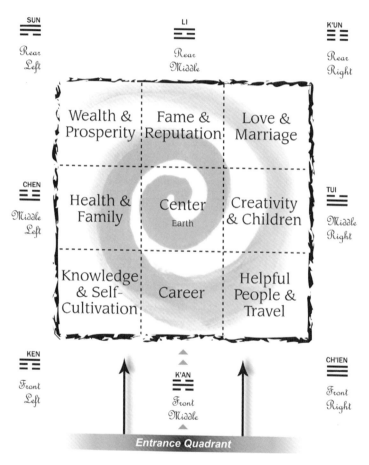

Figure 1A: *The Bagua Map*

Balancing your lifestyle and arranging your home to hold happiness in place are two vital components of Feng Shui. One of the most powerful Feng Shui tools you have to work with is the Bagua Map. The word *Bagua* literally means the "eight trigrams," and they form the basic building blocks of the *I Ching* (the Chinese Book of Changes). Each trigram is associated with a vital aspect of life such as health, wealth, love, and creativity. For instance, you may find that the relationship you cherish—or wish for—is being energized or depleted by the part of your home correlating with Bagua Map's Love and Marriage area. Many people discover that their challenges in life are directly related to the areas in their homes that are disliked, unused, or disorganized.

In one case, the Bagua Map showed that a couple's Love and Marriage area was located in the garage. The wife was quick to realize that the cluttered garage was a perfect metaphor for the "mess" her marriage was in. The reversal of priorities—parking valuable cars outside to make room for the accumulation of used junk—was directly reflected in her marriage. They were essentially parking their relationship outside while they gave the "junk" in their lives all their time and attention. This powerful realization motivated her and her husband to shovel out the garage. It wasn't easy, but as it turned out, organizing the garage to make space for the cars was one of the most romantic things they ever did together. It symbolized their heartfelt desire to bring their relationship home again. As a result, they experienced a delightful resurgence of personal and marital happiness.

When there's something about your life that's mediocre, stressful, or negative, you may experience some upset as a new order is being established. The couple mentioned above certainly did. To reinstate marital bliss, they had to do some hard work to remove the junk that held their mediocre lifestyle in place. Working with the Bagua Map can create some turbulence, as it both reveals and transforms the status quo. Just know that your commitment to happiness will create a new order and a much more enjoyable life.

Mapping Your Home

The Bagua Map can be applied to any fixed shape, including buildings, parcels of property, rooms, and furniture. These instructions will guide you in mapping your home, and once you understand the basics, you can map any structure. You will need a bird's-eye drawing of your home, such as a blueprint or footprint sketch.

- ♥ Determine the overall shape of your home, including all parts that are *attached* to the main house, such as garages, porches, room additions, arbors, storage huts, and decks with railings.

- ♥ Lay the drawing down so that the front entrance of your house is at the bottom of the page (see examples). Use the official front door of your home even if you often use a secondary entrance.

- ♥ Draw a rectangle around your home just big enough to include every part of the home inside it. This is the outline of your Bagua Map.

- ♥ Divide the outline into nine even sections, like a Tic-Tac-Toe board, and label the nine squares according to the Bagua Map in Figure 1A. This is your complete Bagua Map.

When your home is a simple rectangle, you will find that all of the Bagua areas are located inside your house. If your home is any other shape, such as an L, S, T, or U, you'll find areas that are located within the outline of the Bagua Map, but outside the structure of your house. Whether an area is inside or outside, it's very important to determine each area's location, as shown in the following examples:

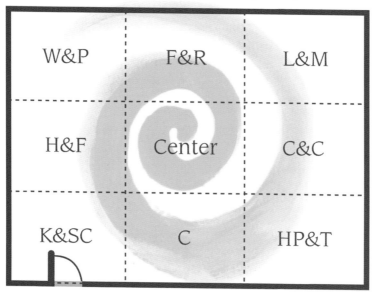

Figure 2A: *This basic sketch of a rectangular home, with its front entrance located in the Knowledge and Self-Cultivation area of the Bagua Map, has all the Bagua areas contained inside the physical structure of the house.*

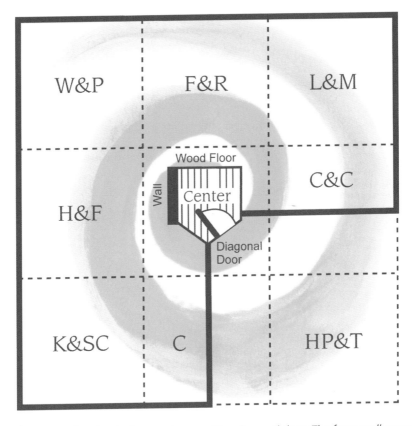

Labels within the figure:

W&P F&R L&M

H&F C&C

Wood Floor
Wall
Center
Diagonal Door

K&SC C HP&T

Figure 3A: *This sketch shows a home with a diagonal door. The foyer wall, wood floor, and direction in which the door opens help determine which way to map the house.*

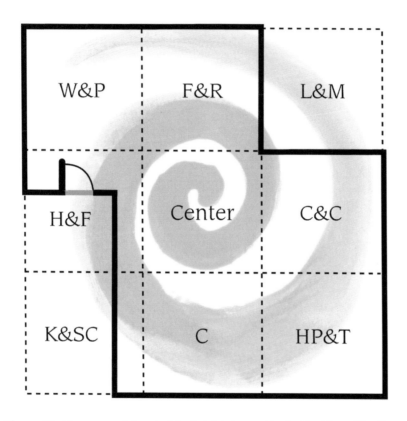

Figure 4A: *The recessed door in this sketch is located in the Health and Family area of this home. Notice that much of the Knowledge and Self-Cultivation, Health and Family, and Love and Marriage areas are outside the structure of the house.*

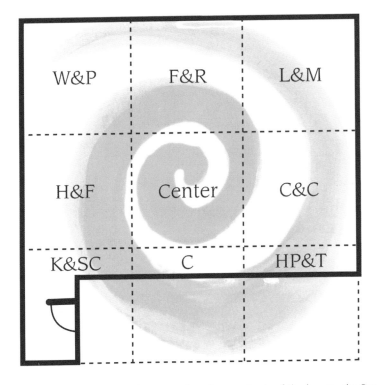

Figure 5A: *When a front door is recessed to the very back of the house, the Bagua Map is turned to fit over the main body of the house, as seen here. Notice that portions of the areas related to Knowledge and Self-Cultivation, Career, and Helpful People and Travel are outside the house's structure.*

Clarifying Points:

1. Don't be concerned with where the interior walls fall inside the map. Sometimes one large room will divide into two or three Bagua areas, or one Bagua area might encompass two or three small rooms.

2. If your home has more than one story, partial or full, the Bagua Map of the main floor will translate up to a second story or down to a lower level. Multiple floors give you multiple opportunities to enhance the Bagua.

3. When the door of your front entrance is built on a diagonal, you will have to "make a call" as to which way to place the Bagua Map on the house. You may have an immediate feeling and intuitively know which way to place the Map. Sometimes, the direction in which tile or carpet has been installed determine the Bagua's direction, as shown in Figure 3A. Other times, the direction you see when you first open the door is the determining factor.

4. When your front door is recessed past the front wall of the house, you may be entering your home through the Health and Family, Center, or Children and Creativity areas of the Bagua Map, as shown in Figure 4A. If your front door is extremely recessed, as shown in Figure 5A, turn the Bagua Map to fit over the main body of the house.

5. Because the home is larger than each room, the changes you make there have more of an immediate impact. Therefore, work first with the Bagua Map of the home, then with the Bagua Map of each room.

6. Consult a Feng Shui practitioner if you need help making a Bagua Map of your home.

Missing Areas of the Bagua Map

When there's a Bagua area located outside the physical structure of your home, it's important to define and enhance that area in some way. This can be as simple as installing an outdoor lamppost, flagpole, ornamental tree, or large statue where the corner would be if the structure were complete. Enhancements such as large boulders, specimen plants, water features, garden furniture, or outdoor sculptures, as shown in the Love and Marriage area of Figure 6A, can also be combined to complete a missing area.

Or, consider the possibility of framing the missing area with a border, fence, or wall, or defining it with a deck, patio, or room addition. The goal is to anchor or complete the missing area with something that enhances the space and is in scale with your home (and your budget).

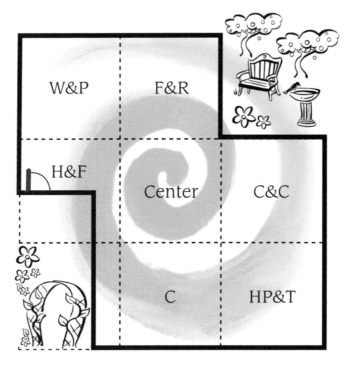

Figure 6A: *The areas outside of the house's structure in Figure 4A have been enhanced here. The Love and Marriage area now includes two ornamental fruit trees, a bench for two, seasonal flowers, and a birdbath. An attractive arbor and border of flowers and plants has also been added to enhance the front entrance and complete the Knowledge and Self-Cultivation and Health and Family areas.*

Personalizing Your Choices

Whenever you can, choose items and designs that relate to the Bagua area you're working with. For instance, if you're working with the Love and Marriage area, you could energize it with one or more of the following:

♥ Two trees, planted appropriately close together, that flower, bear fruit, or have a special growth habit or quality you find attractive.

♥ A garden bench that seats two people, an intimate table with two chairs, and other garden decor in pairs, such as lights, baskets, and flowerpots.

♥ A birdbath, pond, or other water feature with still water to "gather" energy (face a waterfall toward the house and make sure that the design includes a place where the water can pool).

- ♥ Any garden that produces something to gather, such as vegetables, flowers, or herbs.

- ♥ Garden statuary and embellishments that depict twosomes, such as two birds, animals, or people.

Working with the Bagua Map is a very powerful way to create positive change in your life. The objects you choose act as "environmental affirmations," holding your goals and desires in place. The more personally pleasing your choices, the better!

When You Can't Do Anything Sizable Outside

Don't be discouraged if you can't do anything physically substantial to complete a Bagua area outside of your home. There are still many ways you can complete a missing area. You can work with it symbolically outside, inside, or both.

Symbolic Enhancements:

♥ Missing areas can be marked and symbolically strengthened by "planting" a natural quartz crystal to mark the absent corner (see Figure 7A on page 110). Bury the crystal with the point up (or two crystals when you're working with the Love and Marriage area in order to create or strengthen a relationship with another person), an inch or two below the ground with clear intention. Your intention empowers the crystal(s) to energetically strengthen the area that's missing in structure.

- Mark the pavement covering a missing corner with a painted line, circle, or artistic symbol. Again, your clear intention combined with the physical act of enhancing the spot makes your mark powerful.

- Indoors, as shown in Figure 7A, hang a mirror or art depicting an attractive scene on the wall closest to the missing area. This makes the wall "disappear" and symbolically completes the area. Or, use environmental enhancements such as plants, round-faceted crystals, or wind chimes to energize the windows and walls located closest to the absent area.

- Make sure that when an area is missing in your home's structure, you enhance the correlating area in each room of the house. For instance, if the Love and Marriage area is outside the structure of your house, pay special attention to enhancing the Love and Marriage areas in the various rooms of your home.

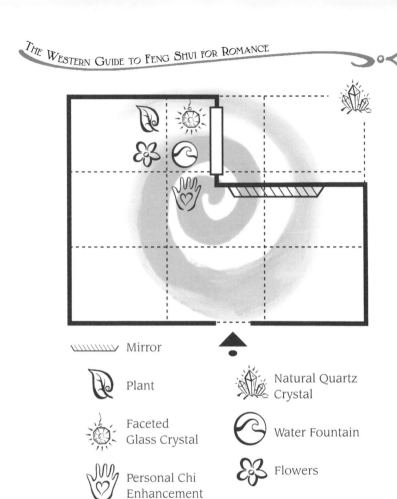

⳾⳾⳾⳾⳾	Mirror		

Plant

Natural Quartz Crystal

Faceted Glass Crystal

Water Fountain

Personal Chi Enhancement

Flowers

Figure 7A: *Use enhancements such as natural crystals, mirrors, art, and plants to add meaning and visual appeal to the indoor locations nearest a "missing" Bagua area.*

Mapping the Bagua in Every Room

Follow the same steps when mapping a room as you did mapping your house. Draw the footprint of the room, place the main entryway at the bottom of the page, draw a rectangle around the perimeter, divide it into nine equal parts, and label each section according to the Bagua Map.

Please note that the Bagua Map of your home and the Bagua Map of each room usually *don't* coincide. Each room has its own smaller Map, with its own possibilities for enhancement. This gives you a Map of your home, plus different smaller Maps for each room.

Assessing Your Bagua Map Profile

Take some time to check out each Bagua area of your home and answer the following questions. Use the same questions to assess the Bagua Map of each room in your house.

- ♥ What room or area is located in each Bagua area?

- ♥ What possessions are located there?

- ♥ Are they organized?

- ♥ Do I like or love everything I see, and what memories and associations do I have with them?

- ♥ Do I see a correlation between what's located in the area and the aspect of my life it corresponds to according to the Bagua Map?

- ♥ Are there improvements I could make?

- ♥ What are the most important improvements or enhancements I need to make right away?

This can be a very revealing process! You may find that the Bagua areas match up with what's working—and what's not working—in your life. Many single people who would like to be in a romantic relationship find that the Love and Marriage areas of their homes are holding their singleness in place. Things change for the better when they remove the "splinters," such as dead plants, art depicting lonely people, or furniture belonging or related to a past flame. The objects you surround yourself with on a daily basis are powerful environmental affirmations and can be holding positive or negative conditions in place. Let your environment be an affirmation of who you are now and all that you're aspiring to be into the future.

The Dance of Yin and Yang Related to the Bagua Map

Ultimately, Feng Shui's Bagua Map leads you to the discovery that all parts of your inner and outer life are interconnected. When you make both character *and* environmental improvements, you're fully aligned with the dance of heart and home, where Yin and Yang are balanced and happiness thrives.

HEALTH AND FAMILY

Related to: The *I Ching* trigram *Chen,* translated as "Shocking Thunder"

Key Attributes: Strength, discernment, and forgiveness

Purpose of Inner Work: To fully enjoy life's many blessings from a strong vantage point that can thrive even during shocking or stressful times

Inner Work: The condition of your physical, emotional, and spiritual health plays a key role in your ability to respond to life's wide spectrum of experiences. The steadfast "care and feeding" of body, heart, and spirit builds your strength to thrive—or survive—in all kinds of circumstances. Inner work focuses on maintaining your soul's well-being by developing the attributes of discernment and forgiveness. Discernment is your inner guardian against weakening influences, supplying you with the 20/20 vision to recognize what builds your strength and what tears it down. Such clear perception empowers you to draw the healthy boundaries that define and protect you. Forgiveness is the self-made magical potion that washes away the burdensome past, freeing you to fully embrace and enjoy the present moment.

Affirmations:

- *I am strong and clear. I attract loving, strengthening influences into my life.*

- *I let go of the past and claim the pure positive potential of this moment.*

- *My body, mind, heart, and spirit are strong and vibrantly healthy.*

Focus on the Health and Family Area When:

- your health needs a boost.

- you're planning, or recovering from, a medical procedure.

- you'd like your social life and your "family of choice" to grow or improve.

- you'd like your relationship with relatives to improve.

- you wish to strengthen the attributes of discernment and forgiveness.

Environmental Enhancements Related to Health and Family:

- ♥ Healthy plants with rounded leaves or a soft, graceful appearance

- ♥ Fresh flowers

- ♥ Dried and silk flowers and plants with a fresh, vibrant appearance

- ♥ Artwork depicting your concept of ideal health

- ♥ Posters and paintings of gardens and landscapes

- ♥ Household decor in floral prints, suggesting vibrant plant life

- ♥ Things made from wood, such as tables, chairs, bowls, and vases

- ♥ Pillars, columns, and pedestals

- ♥ Favorite photos of family and friends

- ♥ Blues and greens

- ♥ Quotes, sayings, and affirmations related to discernment and forgiveness

Wealth and Prosperity

Related to: The *I Ching* trigram *Sun,* meaning "Persistent Wind"

Key Attributes: Gratitude, appreciation

Purpose for Inner Work: To deeply appreciate the wealth of blessings in your life

Inner Work: Consider the many types of abundance that shape your life—your friends, family, health, talents, and memories, to name just a few. Money is only one small part of your overall prosperity. The key is to appreciate abundance in all its forms, knowing that wealth gathers in a grateful pocket. By cultivating an attitude of gratitude, you attune yourself to the full spectrum of wealth. Your appreciation continues to attract riches, adding to your life's portfolio. Revel in the abundance that's yours now, and anticipate it growing with every passing day.

Affirmations:

- *With joy and gratitude, I appreciate the wealth of magnificent people and experiences in my life.*

- *I am rich and prosperous in every way.*

- *I am blessed with a constant and abundant flow of health, wealth, and happiness.*

Focus on the Wealth and Prosperity Area When:

- you wish to generate more cash flow in your life.

- you're raising money or resources for a special purpose.

- you'd like to feel more grateful for the flow of abundance and prosperity in your life.

Environmental Enhancements Related to Wealth and Prosperity:

- ♥ Water features and fountains, symbolizing the abundant flow of resources

- ♥ Wind chimes, prayer flags, and banners that symbolically call in wealth and prosperity

- ♥ Valuable possessions and collections that you love, such as antiques, art, crystal, and coins

- ♥ Posters, paintings, and photographs of the things you'd like to buy or experience

- ♥ All blues, purples, and reds

- ♥ Sayings, quotes, and affirmations related to gratitude and prosperity

FAME AND REPUTATION

Related to: The *I Ching* trigram *Li*, meaning "Clinging Fire"

Key Attributes: Integrity, authenticity, and sincerity

Purpose of Inner Work: To build a reputation of the highest integrity, knowing that it lights your way through the world

Inner Work: The truth is always illuminated in your own heart. When you look within, do you see a person of integrity and authenticity? Do you consider yourself a trustworthy person? Knowing that your reputation lights your way, be mindful that you create a bright future with the thoughts, words, and actions you offer today. While your integrity inspires goodwill and builds bridges to greatness, a lack of it burns bridges and extinguishes your credibility. Let any lack of integrity become a thing of the past, and diligently practice "being your word." This assures an illuminated reputation, cultivates the priceless reward of self-respect, and assures a bright and fortuitous future.

Affirmations:

- 💛 *I am trustworthy in thought, word, and deed.*

- 💛 *My integrity illuminates my path and attracts goodwill and good fortune into my life.*

- 💛 *My authenticity shines brightly in all that I say and do. I trust myself.*

Focus on the Fame and Reputation Area When:

- 💛 you wish to establish a good reputation in your community.

- 💛 you'd like more recognition at work or at home.

- 💛 you'd like to be well known for something you do.

- 💛 you wish to strengthen your practice of integrity and authenticity.

Environmental Enhancements Related to Fame and Reputation:

- ♥ Symbols of your accomplishments, such as diplomas, awards, or trophies
- ♥ Pleasant lighting, symbolizing "illumination"
- ♥ Uplifting artwork that depicts people or animals
- ♥ Items made from (or suggesting) animals, such as leather, faux fur, feathers, bone, and wool
- ♥ Images of people you respect
- ♥ Symbols of your goals for the future
- ♥ Objects or patterns that are triangular or conical in shape, suggesting fire
- ♥ Subtle, bright, and deep shades of red
- ♥ Sayings, quotes, and affirmations relating to integrity and authenticity

LOVE AND MARRIAGE

Related to: The *I Ching* trigram *K'un*, the most Yin of all trigrams, translated as "Receptive Earth"

Key Attributes: Receptivity, pleasure, and romance

Purpose of Inner Work: To be fully open to receiving the pleasures life has to offer

Inner Work: Love grows from the inside out. Its natural evolution begins with self-love, where you prepare a place within to receive the pleasures of loving relationships. Build your capacity to love and be loved by loving yourself *now.* Take the time to "romance" yourself with the same tender, loving attention you'd give a cherished lover, knowing that romance with another person may come and go, but it lasts for a lifetime with yourself. Whether single or married, strengthen your capacity to love by opening your heart fully to yourself, knowing that you are your own true lover and beloved.

Affirmations:

- ♥ *I am a magnificent person. I enjoy an imaginative, creative, romantic life.*

- ♥ *I receive the pleasures of life with open arms.*

- ♥ *I love myself and fill my world with loving thoughts, feelings, and experiences.*

- ♥ *My loving thoughts, words, and actions increase my magnetism and strengthen the heartbeat of joy and happiness within me.*

Focus on the Love and Marriage Area When:

- ♥ you'd like to attract a romantic relationship.

- ♥ you wish to improve the romantic relationship you have now.

- ♥ you're in the process of developing or enriching a loving relationship with yourself.

- ♥ you wish to be more openhearted and receptive

Environmental Enhancements Related to Love and Marriage:

- ♥ Artwork portraying the beauty of romance and love

- ♥ Pairs of things, such as candlesticks, flowers, books, and statues

- ♥ Mementos from happy romantic times

- ♥ Favorite photographs of you, or you and your true love

- ♥ Items in reds, pinks, and white

- ♥ Quotes, sayings, and affirmations on love and romance

CHILDREN AND CREATIVITY

Related to: The *I Ching* trigram *Tui,* meaning "Joyous Lake"

Key Attributes: Joy, ecstasy, and encouragement

Purpose of Inner Work: To "float" in the joyous expression of creativity and to encourage others to do the same

Inner Work: Joy is the primary gateway through which we enter the creative process. The pleasure we take in our offspring, be they children or projects, can connect us with the ecstasy of all creation. Inspire the creative spirit by nurturing yourself and others with generous helpings of encouragement. Watch how you express your creativity, and give yourself more time to do those things that bring you joy. Claim your birthright to be the joyful creator of harmony and beauty in your life. Awaken your creative genius by letting your inner child come out and play, since it's the pure childlike quality of joy within you that opens the door to the creative spirit.

Affirmations:

- *I am a creative genius! I embrace my creativity with great joy and pleasure.*

- *I attract exhilarating people who inspire my creativity.*

- *The more I express myself creatively, the happier I am.*

Focus on the Children and Creativity Area When:

- you're involved in a creative project.

- you feel creatively restricted or blocked.

- you wish to explore and develop your inner-child qualities.

- you'd like to improve your relationship with children.

- you wish to experience more joy and ecstasy in life.

Environmental Enhancements Related to Children and Creativity:

- ♥ Art or objects that are especially creative, whimsical, playful, or colorful, or that stimulate your creative juices

- ♥ Things a child has made by hand

- ♥ Rocks and stones with an inspirational quality

- ♥ Circular and oval shapes

- ♥ Items made from metal

- ♥ Items in white or light pastels

- ♥ Quotes, sayings, and affirmations that apply to joy, children, and creativity

Helpful People and Travel

Related to: The *I Ching* trigram *Ch'ien,* the most Yang of the trigrams, translated as "Heaven"

Key Attributes: Synchronicity, clarity, and confidence

Purpose of Inner Work: To claim your birthright to live a heavenly existence and to allow synchronicity to guide your way

Inner Work: "Heaven on Earth" manifests when you focus clearly on creating a heavenly existence, take action accordingly, and let synchronicity be your guide. Think of the times when you found yourself in the right place with just the right people. This kind of synchronistic experience carries the benevolent power to deliver more heaven to your Earthly experience. When you experience people (including yourself) as angels, and places as paradises, you're in sync with heaven; whereas devilish people and punishing places clearly mark when you're off track. Cultivate clarity of mind, heart, and spirit; set your intentions high and focus upon them; say no to what doesn't match your ideal, and yes to what does. In this way, your brief heavenly forays expand to become your constant experience on Earth.

Affirmations:

- ♥ *Synchronicity guides me to heavenly people and experiences in my life.*

- ♥ *I confidently create my own heaven on Earth.*

- ♥ *I attract the perfect people, places, and things into my life every day.*

- ♥ *I am always in the right place and meeting the right people at the right time.*

Focus on the Helpful People and Travel Area When:

- ♥ you wish to attract more mentors, clients, customers, employees, colleagues—helpful people of any description—into your life.

- ♥ you'd like to travel—either in general—or to a specific place.

- ♥ you're moving to a new home or work location.

- ♥ you wish to experience more synchronicity.

Environmental Enhancements Related to Helpful People and Travel:

- ♥ Art that depicts religious or spiritual figures you love, such as angels, saints, goddesses, and teachers

- ♥ Objects that have personal spiritual associations, such as a rosary, crystal, or book of prayers

- ♥ Photographs of people who have been helpful to you, such as mentors, teachers, or relatives

- ♥ Art, posters, and collages of places you'd like to visit or live, or that are special to you
- ♥ Items in white, gray, and black
- ♥ Quotes, sayings, and affirmations on miracles, heavenly experiences, and synchronicity

CAREER

Related to: The *I Ching* trigram *K'an,* meaning "Deep Water"

Key Attributes: Courage, depth, and trust

Purpose of Inner Work: To develop the courage to dive deep within to discover and align with your soul's purpose

Inner Work: As your career path unfolds, you may be compelled to leave one vocation behind to explore another. This can happen many times as the years roll by and your interests change. Crossing from the familiar to the unfamiliar usually involves a time of "not-knowing," when the soul current is strong and you're immersed in a mystery unfolding. Such a plunge requires courage. You may be required to swim without apparent direction for a while or to buck the current of other people's opinions in order to follow your soul's desire. Your courage and trust are crucial as you let the process of navigating through the unknown carry you along. When you find yourself at a career crossroads, don't hesitate. Plunge in to receive your next set of life instructions. Dream, journal, define your life's purpose, reminisce, and be courageous enough to feel the depths of your own emotions. Wrap yourself in the mystery of life unfolding, knowing that there's treasure awaiting you.

Affirmations:

- ♥ *I trust that every step of my way is soulfully guided.*

- ♥ *I relax and enjoy the process, knowing that my career path reveals itself at the perfect time.*

- ♥ *My work in the world fulfills and inspires me on all levels. I am blessed.*

Focus on the Career Area When:

- ♥ you're seeking your purpose in life.

- ♥ you wish to make a change in your current job or career.

- ♥ you wish to volunteer or do meaningful community-service work.

- ♥ you wish to be more courageous and trusting of life.

Environmental Enhancements Related to Career:

- ♥ Water features such as fountains, waterfalls, and aquariums

- ♥ Artwork or photos depicting bodies of water, such as pools, streams, lakes, or the ocean

- ♥ Images or objects that personally symbolize your career, such as books in your area of expertise, or items with your company name

- ♥ Items that are free-form, flowing, or asymmetrically shaped

- ♥ Items in black or very dark tones

- ♥ Quotes, sayings, and affirmations related to courage and to following one's path in life

KNOWLEDGE AND SELF-CULTIVATION

Related to: The *I Ching's* trigram *Ken,* meaning "Still Mountain"

Key Attributes: Stillness, wisdom, and peace

Purpose of Inner Work: To develop wisdom by taking the time each day to quiet the mind and integrate the experiences of the day

Inner Work: The recipe for wisdom is to blend quiet Yin time with your Yang experiences and activities. A daily practice of meditation, introspection, or contemplation creates the space for the deep integration of life's events. It affords you the time to muse and make new connections that lead to wisdom. Allowing quietude to have a place in your daily routine honors the full rhythm of life and enhances your brilliance, creativity, and productivity. Give yourself a daily gift of stillness. By taking a time-out from being active every waking moment, you find inner peace and deepen the wisdom residing within you.

Affirmations:

- *I am a calm and peaceful presence upon the planet.*
- *My wisdom enhances the world around me.*
- *I embody inner peace and wisdom.*

Focus on the Knowledge and Self-Cultivation Area When:

- you're a student of any subject at any time.
- you're in counseling or engaged in any self-growth activity.
- you wish to cultivate wisdom and peace of mind.

Environmental Enhancements Related to Knowledge and Self-Cultivation:

- ♥ Books, tapes, or other material that you're currently studying
- ♥ Art that portrays mountains or quiet places, such as meditation gardens
- ♥ Pictures or photographs of people you consider accomplished and wise
- ♥ Items in the colors of black, blue, or green
- ♥ Meditative and inspirational sayings, quotes, or affirmations

THE CENTER

Related to: The Center of the Bagua Map, the hub of the wheel, or the "solar plexus" around which life flows

Key Attributes: Being grounded, connected, calm, and centered

Purpose of Inner Work: To remain grounded and centered in daily life and to enjoy a solid connection with the physical earth

Inner Work: Determine how grounded and centered you feel right now. Your connection with the physical Mother Earth strengthens your ability to remain calm and centered through life's many changes. Ground yourself on a regular basis. Fill yourself up with the earth's natural beauty whenever you take a walk or put your hands in the soil. Visualize your connection, and breathe her nurturing energy into your body. Sense your unshakeable connection with the physical earth beneath your feet, and carry it with you wherever you go.

Affirmations:

- ♥ *I am calm, grounded, and centered all the time.*

- ♥ *I carry my connection with the earth with me everywhere I go.*

- ♥ *I am always in the secure and loving embrace of Mother Earth.*

Focus on the Center When:

- ♥ you'd like to feel more calm, grounded, and centered in life.

- ♥ you wish to anchor yourself in a new job or home.

- ♥ you'd like to feel more connected to the natural world.

Environmental Enhancements Related to the Center:

- ♥ Appealing arrangements of items that remind you of your life-giving connection with the earth.

- ♥ Ceramic, earthenware, and tile objects

- ♥ Yellow and earth tones

Appendix B

Taking Romance on the Road

that moving your body from point A to point B can be discombobulating, if not downright stressful. Whether you're moving to a new home, or traveling for business or pleasure, a lot of energy is required. By the time you arrive at your destination, you usually need a rest! This is a great opportunity for self-romance. With a little effort, you can be your own welcoming committee by carrying some atmosphere-makers with you. The ingredients are simple: Select pleasing things that pique your senses, and assemble them in a special box or travel kit. The minute you arrive, you can "let the magic out of the box" and fill the new space with a welcoming atmosphere that's intimately your own.

Here are some suggestions to get you started:

Sight:

- Photos of loved ones (in travel-friendly plastic frames)
- Greeting cards with beautiful inspirational images (lamination extends wear)
- A scarf or other attractive piece of fabric
- A small plastic vase to hold available plant material
- Flowers you send to yourself (include a mushy card)

Touch:

- A pillowcase (or two) that feels wonderful against your skin
- If there's room, an entire set of your favorite linens
- A special lotion that smooths your skin and smells like heaven
- Slippers
- Pajamas, robe, lingerie, or other apparel that dramatically increases your comfort quotient and kinesthetically connects you with home

Smell:

- ❤ A small atomizer (an empty travel hairspray container works well)

- ❤ A small bottle of your favorite essential oil (mix a few drops with water in the atomizer and spray it around the room)

- ❤ Incense

- ❤ A scented candle

Taste:

- ❤ Always travel with water and a good snack!

- ❤ Pack a special picnic, or plan for room service or take-out

- ❤ Some delicious treat, which may or may not be chocolate

Sound:

- Check out the music situation—take a CD player, or find out if the locale provides one
- Mood-enhancing, atmosphere-making CDs and/or tapes
- Small bell or chime
- Earplugs—to minimize noise

Imagine—you've been on the move all day and you finally arrive at your destination. The first thing you do is find a spot that can be a focal point in your new space. It may be the corner of your new bedroom or the top of a hotel bureau. Unfold your scarf and arrange your treasures on it. Kick off the shoes you've worn all day and put on your slippers. Light the candle and incense or spray the room with your favorite scent. Take a long, deep breath and congratulate yourself. Although you may be in a whole new world, you've succeeded in taking the essence of heart and home with you.

ABOUT THE AUTHOR

Terah Kathryn Collins is an internationally recognized teacher, bestselling author, and the originator of Essential Feng Shui®. She is the founder of the Western School of Feng Shui, offering innovative educational programs and services to people around the world.

Over the past 15 years, Terah has studied and collaborated with many Feng Shui teachers, including Dr. Richard Tan, Louis Audet, and Denise Linn. Her extensive background in communications and holistic health merge in her uniquely inspiring perspective and practical approach to Feng Shui, bridging the gap between East and West to effectively produce dynamic, fruitful results.

Featured on the PBS *Body & Soul* TV series, Terah has spoken on Feng Shui to audiences around the globe, including the Magical Mastery and the Today's Wisdom tours in Australia, the New Millennium Conference in Mexico, and the Empowering Women Conferences across the United States.

Terah may be contacted through:
The Western School of Feng Shui
P.O. Box 946, Solana Beach, CA 92075
800-300-6785 or 858-793-0945
www.wsfs.com

If you would like to receive a free catalog featuring additional
Hay House books and products, or if you would like information about the
Hay Foundation, please contact:

Hay House, Inc.
P.O. Box 5100
Carlsbad, CA 92018-5100

(760) 431-7695 or **(800) 654-5126**
(760) 431-6948 (fax) or **(800) 650-5115 (fax)**
www.hayhouse.com

Published and distributed in Australia by: Hay House Australia, Ltd. • 18/36 Ralph St. •
Alexandria NSW 2015 • *Phone:* 612-9669-4299 • *Fax:* 612-9669-4144 •
www.hayhouse.com.au

Published and distributed in the United Kingdom by: Hay House UK, Ltd. • Unit 202,
Canalot Studios • 222 Kensal Rd., London W10 5BN • *Phone:* 44-20-8962-1230 •
Fax: 44-20-8962-1239 • www.hayhouse.co.uk

Published and distributed in the Republic of South Africa by: Hay House SA (Pty),
Ltd., P.O. Box 990, Witkoppen 2068 • *Phone/Fax:* 2711-7012233 • orders@psdprom.co.za

Distributed in Canada by: Raincoast • 9050 Shaughnessy St., Vancouver, B.C. V6P 6E5 •
Phone: (604) 323-7100 • *Fax:* (604) 323-2600

Sign up via the Hay House USA Website to receive the Hay House online newsletter and stay informed about what's going on with your favorite authors. You'll receive bimonthly announcements about: Discounts and Offers, Special Events, Product Highlights, Free Excerpts, Giveaways, and more!